Clara Comstock

"The Orphan Train Lady"

Clara Comstock with two children in Estherville, Iowa.

Front Cover:

Clara Comstock with four Children. Waiting for a wreck to be cleared, Emigration bag in foreground. They appear to be sitting on their luggage, you can see the train tracks to the right.

Clara Comstock

"The Orphan Train Lady"

Steve Cotton

ISBN: 979-8-35097-957-2

Dedicated to those that encouraged me to publish Clara's story into book form.

Contents

Forward

In 2023, the Local History Awareness group chose as its theme "People Who Made a Difference." Various historical societies did exhibits which included a one-room schoolteacher, a missionary, a couple of suffragettes, the founder of The Grange and Clara Comstock, the Orphan Train Lady.

Steve Cotton's exhibit featured four suitably attired orphan manikins, Miss Comstock holding baby Richard Call, pieces of luggage and a train backdrop. Visitors thought it charming until they learned the rational behind the Orphan Train- take unwanted children, clean them up, give them a bible, and put them on a train headed west. At each stop, let prospective families choose the ones they wanted. To 21st century minds, this was a callous, cruel way to deal with helpless, little children who got no say in their futures. The potential for abuse was certainly enormous.

Had this book been available, viewers would have learned the meticulous way Clara Comstock handled placing her orphans in new homes. She gave them much more than "a bath and a bible."

At each stop, a committee of respected citizens vetted families which applied to take children. Every effort was made to place them in homes of the same ethnicity and religion. Siblings were placed together, with related families or very close by. The financial condition and size of homes of each family was considered as was proximity to a school and a church.

The real story comes in reading the case history of each child. By doing a bit of math, the reader will learn how old the child was when they were placed in an orphanage, workhouse or institution, the amount of time they stayed there and their age when they were finally placed with a family. Many were not "helpless, little children." Quite a few were teens at ages that are difficult under the best of circumstances. (2 were 17 when placed!) The large number of families willing to open their homes and hearts to teens from troubled backgrounds will amaze readers. "Intemperate" fathers and "immoral" mothers abound in these stories as well as deceased parents and those who simply abandoned their children.

Taking these stories a few at a time and extracting the details is a rewarding experience.

Clara Comstock managed this program with kindness and compassion producing an overwhelming number of successes.

She certainly did "make a difference" in the lives of hundreds of orphans.

Linda Farris

Acknowledgements

For five years from, 2019 until 2023, I was the Historian for the town of Hartsville located in the southwest part of Steuben County, New York. As a town's historian you get involved in various aspects of the past that shaped our towns into what they are today. In 2016 artifacts from the former Call Museum were dissolved by the Steuben County Historical Society (SCHS). I was invited to be part of the distribution, representing the Kanestio Historical Society (KHS). Housed in the museum was the living room furniture of Clara Comstock. The family that had donated it wanted it to be kept local. After some research on Miss Comstock, I presented to the Board of Directors of the KHS a proposal for them to obtain these pieces and the importance that Miss Comstock played in Hartsville's and Canisteo's local history. To this I am extremely grateful to both the SCHS and the KHS.

Each year the SCHS in cooperation with the Historians and Historical Societies throughout Steuben County holds a History Awareness event in October. The theme changes from year to year. One year it was how the World Wars affected our county, another was agriculture, and in 2023 the theme was about people who made an impact on others. With the knowledge I had gained about Clara Comstock I knew this was the person I wanted to showcase. I dug deeply into Clara's impact on not only her hometown but on the nation and all the children she helped in her career. The topic for the 2023 awareness week I thought was tough at first, therefore I owe thanks to the committee that select the topic. Without it, this book wouldn't have been possible.

In my quest to link stories of children either placed in Steuben County or taken west from the county, I've met many contributors that help paint the picture of Clara. First and most importantly was her niece, Natalie Comstock Cobb. Who provided me with family material on who her aunt was.

Local information regarding families affected by Clara's work to whom I'm extremely grateful for sharing their stories are Mary Burg, Nancy Harding, Roseanne Testani Wall, Connie Mullen. (Hope I didn't miss anyone, if so, I apologize.)

Also, thanks to our new county Historian, Griffin Bates, and the SCHS, along with the staff at the Finger lakes Boating Museum in Hammondsport, N.Y. for all you do to help preserve histories such as this one.

A special thanks is extended to Linda Farris, retired teacher, for not only her help with the Clara Comstock display during the 2023 History Awareness Week, but for her proofreading skills and forward. Her friendship and skills were greatly appreciated in making this work happen.

Thanks to my fellow high school classmate and Wheeler, N.Y. Historian, Cindy Norton, for her graphic design skills in helping with the cover design of this book.

Introductions

The movement spanning 74 years is, without a doubt, a period in American history where a great migration of underaged children were placed with respectable families through Midwest. Clara Comstock became a Children Aid Society (CAS) agent toward the end, beginning her career in 1911 running for the last 17 years. This writing focuses on Miss Comstock's involvement and explores the history behind some of "her children".

The stories in this writing are not intended to offend anyone or disclose family secrets. After all it's been almost a century since the last train ran in 1928.

The "Orphan Train" movement began in 1854 to help find homes for children that were living on the streets of New York City. In 1850 there was an estimated 30,000 homeless children mostly of new immigrants from poor and destitute families. The "Children's Village", "Children Aid Society" (CAS), and the "New York Foundling Hospital" were institutions that developed programs to place the homeless, orphaned, and abandoned children in homes throughout the Midwest.

The "The Children's Village" was established in 1851 by 24 Philanthropists. The "CAS" founder was by Charles Loring Brace forming in 1853. While the "New York Foundling Hospital" was formed by the Sisters of Charity where they would receive infants along with unwanted children whose parents could no longer provide proper care for them.

At first some of the midwestern farmers were taking in children for farm labor. Once this was determined Mr. Brace made sure the CAS workers followed up with the children throughout their childhood to ensure that the children were being cared for and not just free labors.

The term "Orphan Train" didn't catch on until after the era but was originally known by the Catholic Orphanages as the "Mercy Train". These trains were the founding of the modern foster care movement. Pursuing a humanitarian solution to the impoverished lives the children were living on the streets.

The support often came from individuals who were either wealthy and made donations or from generous donations in estate settling such as this one:

> The "Bath Advocate" newspaper dated March 27, 1912; under the section of Surrogate's Proceedings, we learn that John McGrath who resided at the Veterans

Administration facility appointed Rev. John Farrell as the executor of his estate. Rev. Farrell will receive $50; with the balance of $718 to be divided between two institutions that provide homes for orphan children. The executor to choose which two institutions will receive the funds.

This article was published in the Batavia, New York article from April 29, 1924, it reads: "Miss Comstock of Hornell Orphanage was in town last week looking for homes for children."

You will read in this writing a distance referred to as "a rod" such as someone lives 40-rods from the local school. For reference, "a rod" is equal to 16.5 feet.

A flag indicates that once grown the child entered into the military.

Reading Clara's notes there are cases where a boy is placed in a home who had all girls. And in cases, where a girl in a home where the family had all boys.

There are a few cases in these notes such as Mr. Applequest of Hepburn, Iowa where the system worked, and he took in multiple children over the years. In 1911 he took in a twelve-year-old child, then in 1915 a nine-year-old, and in 1918 a ten-year-old.

Clara Comstock was inducted into the Steuben County Hall of Fame in 2017. Her legacy that she left on the world will live on in the county history.

Chapter 1   History of the orphan train movement

History of the Orphan Train:

- The Orphan Train operated from 1854 until 1928. An estimated 280,000 children were relocated. Mostly in the mid-western states.

- Children's Aid Society (CAS) office was on East Twenty-Second Street in New York City

- The children were nervous, for they were about to embark on a life-changing journey, but Miss Comstock was undoubtedly confident and put them at ease.

- After all the CAS was established to provide for the poor, abandoned, and neglected children living on the streets of NYC. The Rev. Charles Loring Brace established the Brace Memorial Farm School emphasizing the importance of self-help. The school believed that the best way to help the children was to establish a network of industrial schools. Schools that would provide the children's basic needs and were fundamental in providing instructions in Reading, Writing, and Mathematics and Occupational Skills.

- They taught the girls sewing, dressmaking & hat making, domestic skills such as cleaning and cooking, while teaching the boys carpentry, shoemaking, and farming. By 1900 the city had 2,500 successful industrial schools in the city.

- The children needed a second chance, Miss Comstock along with other CAS workers would accompany the children to towns where good, respectable people would take them in, make them part of their family and provide them with the chance of a better life.

- The CAS workers would interview prospective families. After a week would re-evaluate their decision, talking separately to the child and the new parents. If it wasn't a good fit, they would pull the child out of that home and place them with another family, either in that community or the next one down the rail line.

- Each year, the Agent from the CAS that placed a child followed up until the child turned 18 years of age to ensure things were acceptable in the household.

Chapter 2   Clara Comstock, "The Orphan Train Lady"

Clara Comstock 1879 – 1963

Clara Comstock grew up in Hartsville, born July 5th, 1879, to Charles and Charity Comstock. She had a brother, Daniel, two years younger. Her father made a living as a farmer and blacksmith. Clara graduated from the Canisteo Academy in 1895 at the age of sixteen. She went on continuing her education at the Academy's Teacher Training Course. The Teacher Training Course requirements were you had to be at least 17 years of age and have a twenty-eight academic count in specific subjects. The training course lasted one to two years depending on the student's progress.

The teaching certificate was valid for three years. If you taught for two out of three years, the certificate was renewed for five-year periods and was good for a lifetime if you continuously taught. The training certificate was good for teaching at the elementary and grade school level.

Clara began her teaching career in the fall 1898 in District number 5 (right) in Hartsville with the weekly salary of $7.00. Leaving Hartsville in 1903, she started a new career at the Brace Memorial Farm

School in Valhalla, Westchester County just north of New York City (NYC).

Brace Memorial Farm School paid her a salary of $40.00 per month and provided her with room and board. The school was a 150-acre farm that taught homeless boys between the ages of 10 to 16 useful farm skills. They were taught agricultural, literacy and life skills, along with personal hygiene and basic manners. Arrangements would be made for them to go South or West to be employed on farms.

Here are four postcards of the Bryce Farm School in Valhalla, N.Y. That Clara worked as a teacher for eight years.

Clara worked eight years at the Farm School and then in 1911 moved to NYC to begin working as an agent for the Children's Aid Society (CAS); here's where she became known as **"The Orphan Train Lady"**, a title that stuck with her, her entire life.

Her job was to select adoptable children from NYC orphanages and escort them by train to destinations west.

Between 1854 and 1929 it's estimated that 290,000 children road the orphan train. Between 1911 and 1928 Clara escorted seventy-four groups of children herself.

As an agent for the CAS, her duties included selecting children for the journey. Children would be washed, given a haircut, and a new set of clothes for traveling and a second set of clothes for presentation to a potential set of parents. The agent would purchase group tickets as they would be cheaper for the train ride out of NYC. They would bring along provisions and buy only fresh fruit and milk at the local whistle stops along the route.

They would attend to both the physical and emotional needs of the children. Clara was stern when necessary and never held a grudge. She was "Sweet & Motherly" and provided compassionate guidance.

For the most part the children were placed in homes in the Mid-West; none were ever placed past the Rocky Mountains.

To find a suitable town for placement the following had to be met: the town had to be on an established train route with a population of between three to four thousand inhabitants. The town had to be located in a thriving farmland region and have good schools and a nearby college.

The agents would select a location for a reception; have a public announcement made, organize a committee of local businessmen to screen potential foster parents. The committee would consist of the following members; **Banker** – (or someone with a financial background), **Minister**, (for church life), **Doctor** (he would know if a family was under stress), **Retired Farmer** (who would know the community), a **Lawyer** and a **Merchant** (for their business life), and the **Editor** of the local newspaper (he was considered the most important member of the committee).

The group would leave NYC usually on a Tuesday afternoon, reaching their destination by Friday. The children would then get cleaned up and change their clothing. Potential parents would meet them at such places as the local church, hotel, or even opera house. If the agent saw a suitable match and the child was willing, the necessary paperwork would be drawn up for the new family.

On Saturday and Sunday, the agents would follow-up by hiring a local livery to drive them to visit the families and children where they were placed. Following the home visits, the agent drafted detailed reports which were mailed back to NYC. Each trip took two weeks to complete.

Preparing for the trip:
- The babies always called forth the most interest, this interest helped place the older children, so they tried to take a baby with each party.
- Brothers and sisters were placed together, or in the same neighborhood so that they saw each other frequently.
- The Children would be placed in homes with their same ethnicity and religion. So, an Irish child would be placed with an Irish family. A child whose family was Presbyterian was placed with a Presbyterian family.
- Each child was given two changes of clothing, hat, coat, gloves, and a Bible. The girls were given a nice silk or wool dress. The thought was that the children must look as well-groomed as those of the children in the community where they were to go.
- Huge trunks were checked; an emergency bag was taken out for the trip. The Emergency bag contained knives, forks, and spoons, along with bibs, towels, washcloths, soap, toothpaste & toothbrushes, a sewing kit, and medicine for colds, coughs, burns, etc. A Sterno Burner to heat milk for the babies along with blankets and knitted shawls for the babies were included.
- The agent took their personal trunks, as they might be in the west for a week or several months and had to be ready to travel at a minute's notice.
- Most trips they would occupy the backseats of a coach. With larger groups, sometimes a separate coach would

be added to the train for them. Trips usually last 3- or 4-days changing trains in Chicago or St. Louis.

- Food was seldom purchased along the route but taken with them on the trip. The food lockers would contain loaves of graham and white bread and sandwich fillings such as Ham & Cheese and Peanut Butter & Jelly. They also took along Lettuce, Celery, Mayonnaise, Figs, Dates, Raisins, Apples, Oranges, Bananas, Cakes, Cookies, and Condensed Milk.

Anna Laura Hill: another Orphan Train agent from Elmira, N.Y. worked for the CAS and became an associate of Clara Comstock. The two ladies remained friends their entire life.

Pictured below is Miss Hill:

Retirement: Clara escorted the last group of orphans in 1928. She then worked as the superintendent of the CAS until her retirement in 1944. She retired to Collier Street in Hornell, N.Y.

Clara was a member of the Daughters of the American Revolution (DAR) where she was the regent from 1935 – 1937. She was credited as the founder of the Canisteo Valley Genealogical and Historical Society.

She carefully selected families for more than 12,000 homeless/orphaned children. She stayed in contact with each and every one of them until they reached adulthood.

In retirement she continued to follow-up with children in the Western New York region. She never held a driver's license, hiring her brother after retirement to escort her to see "her children". She died on September 11, 1964, and is buried in the Hornellsville Rural Cemetey.

Pictured: 1912, 1913, & 1914 Train Passes.

Chapter 3   Local Stories

In the history awareness display (mentioned earlier) five children were showcased. Four of the five children had a connection to Steuben County. The exception was the "Orphan Mayor", an orphan that ended up being the mayor of Kansas City, Kansas. These are their stories as if they were telling them.

Elise May (Turner) Roberts

My mother died when I was young and I was sent to live with my Grandparents, Charles & Susan Cobb, who lived in Adrian, NY. My father then married my aunt, and to them was born my half sister Mary Elizabeth. My sister and I were put on the train in Hornell, NY where Miss Clara Comstock took us on the Orphan Train to Fredonia, Kansas. In Fredonia I lived with my foster parents until I married Earl M. Roberts when I was 18 years old. Earl and I had a son the following year. (Due to illness, Elise May died at the age of twenty.)

Mary Elizabeth (Turner) (Bounds) Ratley

With my dad being a traveling entrepreneur, momma no longer could care for me. Grandma Cobb put my sister Elise May and me on the train in Hornell, NY. We were placed in two different homes in Fredonia, Kansas. Being we lived in the same town we could see each other often. I was adopted by Clarence and Ora Bounds, married Erenst Ratley and became a registered nurse. Erenst and I moved to Wichita, Kansas. In Wichita I worked at St. Francis hospital. During the polio pandemic from 1948 until 1955 I worked with patients in the "Iron Lungs" unit. (After retirement, Mary Ratley lived to be seventy-seven.)

Elise and Mary had another sister; her whereabouts is not known. Mary, however, kept in contact with her New York family over the years.

Pictured: Mary Ratley pictured in the Iron Lung Unit of St. Francis Hospital.

Henry Lee Jost

(Mr. Jost's story isn't local to Steuben County, however he is showcased here as he was part of the History Awareness display 2023.)

My mother died when I was young, and my ailing father could no longer care of me, I was sent to the orphanage until I rode the train westward to Hopkins, Missouri. I moved to Kansas City, Kansas when I was old enough to attend law school. After law school I became the Jackson County prosecuting attorney. Served two terms as Mayor of Kansas City where I gained the nickname of the "Orphan Boy Mayor." I then served one term as a United States Congressman before returning back to Kansas City to continue law practice. (Mr. Jost was married and had two children. He died at the age of seventy-six.)

Rev. Dr. Dan B. Brummitt

I was born in England and came to the United States when I was a teenager. Shortly afterwards my parents died, I was sent to the Orphanage and road the train to Kansas. I was adopted by a doctor and his wife. I graduated from Baker University in Baldwin, Kansas and from Drew University in Madison, New Jersey. I was the Head of the Christian Advocate in the Mid-West. Editor and author of the Epworth League Methods. Served as the Northwestern Christian Advocate for the Methodist Church and a noted guest speaker, speaking in the region including in Hornell, NY. (Mr. Brummitt died at the age of seventy-one leaving behind his widow and one son.)

Richard Call

My parents immigrated from Holland. My father died in an automobile accident just before I was born. My mother, on a housekeeper's salary, was unable to care for me. She sent me to the Orphanage  where Miss Comstock selected me for a family in her hometown of Hartsville, NY. I rode the orphan train and was adopted by William Call and his wife, Issabelle. They had already adopted a little girl, my new sister, Bernice. When my new mom died, dad married Myra Stephens who was my schoolteacher. I went into the army in 1944 until 1956 serving in Korea and the Philippines. After the army I worked at the VA center in Bath, NY, as head of prosthetics. I was the Historian of Hartsville and opened up a museum there. When I was an adult, I found my

birth mother Canandaigua, N.Y. in an apartment with her sister. I was able to purchase a duplex where my mother could live on one side and her sister on the other. (Mr. Call died at the age of seventy-eight.)

Pictured: Bernice & Richard

Other Local Stories.

Samual John Geleta

I was born in 1902 at the Infant Asylum in New York City. I rode the orphan train in 1903, where the Hoes family took me in. My new mother died, and I was taken in by another family. As the result of a farming accident, I injured my leg. The local physicians thought I'd lose the leg unless I could go back to a New York City Hospital. I spent over a year in the NYC Hospital. My leg healed, but I always walked with a limp. At the age of 12 I was then placed by Miss Comstock with Mr. and Mrs. Alfred Hathaway in Cameron, N.Y. Mr. Hathaway was a postal worker. As a teen I delivered papers in Cameron for a half cent per paper.

As an adult I came to Hornell, N.Y. to work for the Erie. First as a seal inspector then became a brakeman.

Sam; 1st row far right.

Billy Montgomery

My parents died when I was six months old in 1880. When I was one, I was taken to Bradford, Pennsylvania to be adopted. I was adopted by Thaddeus and Nettie Clarkson. Thus took the name of William (Will) Clarkson.

The Clarkson's were originally from the town of Sullivan, Madison County, N.Y. My new mom, Nettie's maiden name was Clark. The Clarkson's married in 170 and were childless when they adopted me in 1881. For employment reasons, my new dad moved to Oil Town, Pennsylvania, then to Kane where they lived until Mettie died in 1889.

My dad and I moved first to Andover, N.Y. In 1893 Thaddeus's brother Edger and he went into business together, moving us to Canisteo, known as E. Clarkson & Bro. They ran a Merchandise and Grocery store. Edger's wife opened a Millinery Store.

Pictured: single story structure to the right was the Millinery Store, two story to the left was the Merchandise and Right the Grocery.

My dad, Mr. Thaddeus Clarkson, married the widow Sarah (Mullen) Flohr in Sarah's living room parlor. At the age of 15 I began to pilfer (to Steal, especially in small quantities) about dad's store. I was then sent to my uncle David Clarkson in Troupsburg to work as a farm hand.

Two weeks later I came up missing and turned up in Olean, N.Y. where George Myrick from Olean returned home from church only to find me, Will Clarkson, hiding in their house behind a curtain. I admitted I was there to burglarize them.

I ended up in show business doing variety shows, known in show business by my birth name, Montgomery. In 1911 I was making as much as $1,500 a week. I first married fellow actresses, Florence Moore, and second Minnie Allen.

William (Clarkson) Montgomery died at the age of 54, he had no children.

Published in the Andover newspaper we find the following article:

"William Montgomery, a stepson of Mr. and Mrs. T.M. Clarkson of Andover, plans to take the whole Clarkson family, numbering some 30 members, to Washington state next year to the home of a relative for the annual reunion. Montgomery is an actor. He will charter a private coach for the party."

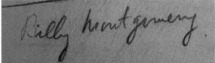

Billy's Agent's photo and signature used by his agent.

1914 Sheet Music Montgomery and Moore.

1912 Sheet Music Montgomery and Moore.

Other Steuben County Stories

Leon Floyd Hodge

In Chapter 5, Clara's Notes, page 74 of this book we find the following note.

Leon Floyd Hodge, case number 8557, was born in Corning, N.Y. on April 14, 1907. His parents were Floyd and Louise (Dixon) Hodge. He had a sister Frances Hodge. Leon was surrendered by his mother to the Poor Master, Corning, N.Y. on August 3, 1912. He was taken in by Robert W. Smith who lived thirteen miles north of Decorah, Iowa in Mabel, Minnesota. The Smiths lived three quarters of a mile from the local school and owned an 80-acre farm.

Leon's Story: His sister Frances died 1909/10 was less than a year old and is buried in the Corning Hope Cemetery in New York State. He had five additional siblings. Their last name is Havens, A brother, Claude, born 1916/17, an electrician contractor by trade and lived in Columbia, Missouri. Four Sisters, Lillian Havens, who lived with Leslie and Lola Forbis in the city of Rural, Broone County, Missouri. Lillian was born January 30, 1923, and married Milton Loyd, they resided also in Columbia, Missouri. Three other sisters, Blanch, Florence, and Rose Havens. In 1958 at the time of Louise's death Blanch was married, her married name is Burgess and living in Corning, N.Y. Florence's married name is Ashteneau, residing in Detroit, Michigan. And Rose married name is Wallace living in Newark, N.Y.

Leon served his country in the Navy during WW II. He moved back to Corning, N.Y., residing at 206 Park Avenue, where his mother moved into his household. Louise after a short illness died in the Corning Hospital at 7:55pm on Thursday, December 11, 1958.

Helen and Margaret Miles

In Chapter 5, Clara's Notes, page 93 of this book we find the following note.

Helen Miles, case number 9116, was born in Rathbone, N.Y. on December 24, 911.

Margaret Miles, case number 9117, was born on January 15, 1910.

Their parents were Orson and Anna B. (Covel) Miles. Orson was a farmer from Rathbone, N.Y. and Helen was from Bath, N.Y. Their mother turned them over to the CAS.

Helen was placed in the home of Sigmund Frederick and Mary Schirmer who lived four-blocks northwest of the depot in Mt. Vernon, S.D. Her new family was of the Methodist faith owning their own house near the school. Mr. Frederick worked as a banker.

Margaret was placed with Thomas Nerland on March 19, 1914, who lived eighteen miles from Ru Heights, S.D.

Helen's and Margaret's story: Orson Miles of Rathbone, N.Y. was 42 years old in 1904. His fiancé Anna Covill was 15 years old residing in Sunderlandville, Pa. They went on August 31 to the Rathbone Methodist parsonage requesting Rev. E.D. Compton to speak the words that would make them husband and wife. Due to the difference in age the Rev. Compton declined to perform the ceremony.

The couple proceeded to Addison with Anna's mother, where her mother lied and gave her daughter's age as 18. Where the two were united in marriage.

Following issues in the marriage, in March of 1914 Anna turned the girls over to the Children's Aid Society.

Elmira

These following children were picked up from the Elmira area just east of Steuben County. In Chapter 5, Clara's Notes, of this book, we find their cases.

Chapter 4   Love and Humanity

The following article was published in the Andover, New York newspaper dated May 16, 1913. The seven Slater children were picked up at the **Five Point House** of Industry in Oxford, N.Y. in Chenango County just north of Binghamton; the three Kinney children and two Havens, from **United Helpers Home** in Ogdensburg, N.Y. in the North Country along the St. Lawrence Seaway.

Twelve Orphans Given Homes

Andover Woman Goes with and Cares for Party of Homeless Children Routed to South Dakota

Mrs. Maude Prest arrived home the last week from a trip with Miss Clara Comstock, agent of the New York Children Aid Society. They had been in Canton, South Dakota, with a party of children. The following is from the Sioux Falls News:

Twelve orphans, boys and girls, ranging from the age of four to sixteen years old were brought to this city from New York on Friday by representatives of the Children Aid Society of New York, and as a result eight homes in Canton and vicinity were brightened with the sunshine of childhood life, and twelve boys and girls thrown into the world through the death of their parents and the inability of relatives to care for them, have found places where they may be given loving care, Christian training and education, the three essential requirements for truly useful citizens. The request of the Society for homes for these children found a ready response in the hearts of the people of Canton and when they arrived at the Opera House on last Friday afternoon, they found the audience crowded with respectable citizens of the community ready to welcome the homeless ones and take them in as their own.

Miss Anna Laura Hill, one of the representatives of the society, gave a short address in which she explained the work of the society and set forth the plan for distributing the children. Miss Clara Comstock then gave the names and ages of the children and told at least a part of their particulars.

The children were not distributed on the "first come, first served" plan but applications were taken, over thirty in all, and each was given careful consideration by the ladies in charge of the children, assisted by a committee of local people. The children were placed in homes considered to be best fitted in their natures. The following are the names and ages of the children and the homes in which they were assigned:

Eunice Slater, age 16, to Professor and Mrs. H. M. Dale.

Margaret Slater, age 15, and Lemuel Slater age 5 to Mr. and Mrs. Charles Johnson.
Lillie Slater, age 9, and Catherine Slater, age 4 to Mr. Mrs. Oral Hudson

Raymond Slater, age 11, to Mr. and Mrs. A. H. Chappell.

William Slater, age 13, to Mr. and Mrs. W. N. Searle.

Arland Kinney, age 9 and. Una Kinney, age 7, to Mr. and Mrs. A.C. Johnson

Violet May Kinney, Age 12, to Mr. and Mrs. Gordon Ellis

Charles Haven, age 9, and Ethel Marion Havens, age 8, to Mr. and Mrs. Sam Thorson

A great many went to the Opera House out of curiosity, expecting to see a crowd of typical street waifs, ragged and unkempt. in other words, a pack of heathens. What they really found was twelve bright eyed, intelligent American boys and girls, with traces of good breeding showing in their every feature. The appearance of the little band excited the admiration and won the love of all. It was evident from the first that they would not want homes, and the only problem was the placing of the little tots in the homes best suited for their nature and fancies. That the committee succeeded in the greatest measure is proven by a list of assignments given above. It is the hope and wish of all the people of our city that the little orphans may find in their new homes all the comforts and love so necessary to ideal children's life and it is the belief of all that such will be the case. The foster parents of these little ones are to be congratulated and commended for the love and humanity that has prompted this showing of interest in the welfare of these future citizens of this great country.   Sioux Valley News, South Dakota.

The Slater family:

Edward Slater, Sr. emigrated to this country from England where he was born in 1839. His wife Margaret was born the same year, census records indicate she was born in North Carolina while some list her as being born in Tennessee. The two married before 1865 and settled in Castleton, Richmond County, Staten Island, New York.

Edward Sr's. parents migrated to the United States sometime between 1850 and 1855. His father William, a laborer, was born in 1815, his mother Elizabeth in 1814. He had two siblings, a brother Racub born 1844 and a sister Eunice born 1848.

Edward Sr., a civil war veteran, found work as a painter to support his growing family. To the union were born the following children. Edward Jr. 1866, William 1869, Lemuel 1872, and Irving 1875. Census records show both Edward and Lemuel were born in Richmond County. However, the 1875 census indicates that William was born in Jersey City while Irving was born in Virginia according to the 1875 & 1880 federal census records.)

Edward Sr. died prior to 1900 as we find his wife Margaret living with Lemuel and his family and listed as a widow.

Lemuel married his wife Catherine prior to 1897. To them were born seven children. Eunice 1897, Margaret 1898, William 1900, Raymond 1902, Lillian 1904, Lemuel 1908, and Catherine 1909. Mr. Slater dies in 1909.

Unfortunately, mom, Catherine, dies and the children are left with Grandma. Due to the decline in grandma, Margaret's, health she is placed in the "Women's Relief Corps", (W.R.C.), a.k.a. NYS Veteran's Home in Oxford, N.Y. just north of Binghamton in 1913. The W.R.C. is the auxiliary of the Civil War Grand Army of the Republic. The children are placed in the "Five Point House of Industry" in lower Manhattan.   Clara Comstock pulled the pages out of her logbook children that became of age. We find the two oldest girls, Eunice and Margaret's pages had been removed from the log. However, the five younger children's pages remained in the book.

Five Pint House of Industry, New York City

William, case number 8717, is placed in Canton, S.D., RFD 5 which is five miles west and one and a half south of the railroad depot arriving on May 10th, 1913. He is placed in the home of Fred Mample who owns an eight-room farmhouse of 370 acres. Mr. Mample has one child of his own living just one mile from the school.

Raymond, case number 8716, is also placed in the Canton area also in the RFD 5 district but four miles north and three and a half miles west of the depot. William's guardian was Thomas Newborn, a farmer, with a six-room farmhouse on 320 acres one mile from the local school.

Lillian, case number 8714, joins Ode & Helmina Nordlie's family on May 10th, 1913. The Nordlie's live in Hudson, S.D., nine miles west and eleven miles south of the depot in Canton. Mr. Nordlie is a Lutheran with a nine-room farmhouse situated on 320 acres. He has two children, a son Obed J. aged fifteen and a daughter Thelma aged thirteen residing one and a half miles from the local school.

Lemuel, case number 8713, is located in the town of Alcester, S.D. eight miles northwest of the Canton railroad depot. Oscar J. & Mabel M. Monson takes him home to a seven-room farmhouse sitting on 160 acres 1 ¾ files from the school. The Monsons are of the Lutheran faith. Oscar's sister Nora also lives with them.

Catherine, case number 8711, joins the same household as her sister Lillian.

Margaret went to nursing school in Dell Rapids, Minnehaha, S.D. Raymond and Lemuel returned back east, Raymond lived on Horace Avenue, Roosevelt on Long Island, while Lemuel lived in Plymouth, N.H. Catherine moved to Sioux Falls, S.D. It's not sure the path the other three children led.

The Kinney family:

The Otis Kinney family operated one of the "Lockie Farms" in Elmdale north of Watertown, NY. Mr. Kinney developed a cancer of the face which forced him to give up farming and move his family to Gouverneur. Losing the battle on Sunday morning, September 28th, 1912, after spending two months in the county house near Canton before being transferred to St. John's hospital. He alternated between farming and teaming (driving coal wagons) throughout the years.

Otis and his wife, Lettie Anna Ellwood married on September 30th, 1885, in the town of Russell, St. Lawrence County, N.Y. Otis was the son of Benjamin Kinney and Lydia Willard. He was born in 1864. Lettie, the daughter of William Ellwood and Katherine Dana was born in 1866. To this union was born eight children. Seven of the children are: Lovell J. 1890, Lionel W. 1893, Lyndon O. 1897, Bryan W. 1899, Violet M. 1901, Arland A. 1903, and Unabelle B. 1906. One child (name and year born are unknown) was in an institution for feeble minded children in Rome, N.Y.

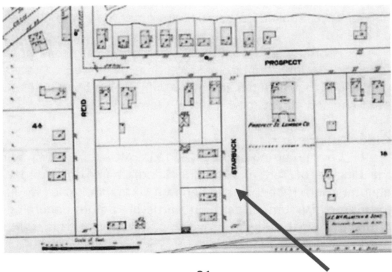

Lettie, with the three youngest children lived on Starbuck Street in Gouverneur. The oldest son, Lovell, was married, while the other three boys, ranging in age from 15 to 20, were out of the house employed on local farms. It had been reported that Lettie had been acting strangely for some time since her husband had died. On January 30th, 1913, she was committed to the St. Lawrence State Hospital after being adjudged insane by Doctors Samuel W. Case and Stanley W. Sayer. The younger three children were turned over to Henry Lang, Overseer of the Poor. Mr. Lang took them to the United Helpers Home in Ogdensburg.

Leading up to having Mrs. Kinney committed to the state hospital; with temperature well below zero she walked with the children over a mile to the Methodist parsonage and aroused the pastor, Rev. W. M. Hydon. Telling him there was someone about her house and she was afraid to stay there. Rev. Haydon took her and the children to St. Lawrence where he paid for lodging for them for the night. The chief of police spent time at the Kinney home and found no one. Mrs. Kinney told them where he would find some of her belongings. Items found along the "WYE" of the RW&O railroad (Rome, Watertown, and Ogdensburg) included a Bible, jewelry, and a dictionary. In a nearby field other rubbish was found.

The oldest girl, Violet, could have been left in the care of family, however, it was decided not to separate them as there might have been a chance mom would recover. If so the three would return to her care. One of the sons took charge of the house, it was locked up pending the outcome of the mother's condition.

February 11th, 1928, Lettie fell down the stairs of the Jefferson County Sanitarium fracturing her instep. She was released in the car of her son Byron with the aid of crutches. By 1930 she had moved in with Lionel's family.

Older Children:

Lovell married on June 26, 1912, Miss Eliza W. Chapin, the daughter of Frank and Emeline (Reed) Chapin. Thay had two children, Ivan H. Chapin, and Kenneth E. Chapin. Lovell worked for a time at a lumber camp in Harrisville before becoming a farmer living in the Edwards township. Lovell served his country during World War I. He died March 28, 1963, and is buried in the Fowler Cemetery.

Lionel married twice. His first wife was named Irene, to them were born two daughters, Esther and Eliza. He second married Gertrude High who had two children from a previous marriage, a son and daughter, Franis J. and Gertrude M. Lionel was 20 years old when his mother was institutionalized and working on a farm. Lionel and his family lived in Gouverneur, N.Y.

Lindon, sometimes referred to as Lincoln, resided for a time in Cazenovia, Gouverneur, and Potsdam, before moving to Oswegatchie Trail, Star Lake, N.Y. Lindon married Marjorie B. Nichols on July 29, 1918, by Rev. Rhodes of Cazenovia. Marjorie was the daughter of George R. and Theo Nichols. To them were born five children, George R., John B., Lincoln (Lindon) Jr., May, and Helen. Lindon was 16 years old when his mother was institutionalized and working on a farm. Lindon worked as a farmer before retirement and died on September 28th, 1968.

Bryan and his wife Susan had two sons and five daughters. Their sons are Alwin and Forrest, daughters Janice, Violet, Etta, Frances, and Unabelle. Bryan was 15 years old when his mother was institutionalized and working on a farm. Living in Fowler and farming he worked 31 years for the Loomis Tale Co., before moving to Oxbow where he worked for the town of Antwerp before retiring in 1960. He died on August 6, 1979, at the age of eighty-one.

Younger three children:
Violet is the only one of the three whose page remains in Miss Comstock's logbook. Presumably, the page for the other two was pulled out and assigned to another CAS agent at some time. As mentioned earlier, the children were placed with the United Helpers Home in Ogdensburg, N.Y. Due to circumstances, it had been decided that the three younger children would be better if kept together. However, once they were placed on the Orphan Train and arrived in South Dakota Violet was placed in a different home, over a hundred and sixteen miles from the younger two.

Violet, case number 8710, was born May 2nd, 1901, in Gouverneur, N.Y. childhood diseases included whooping cough and measles. She was first road the train in 1913 with her younger siblings. There is no record of where she was placed. However, three years later on May 15, 1916, she was placed in the home of Mrs. Robert McCue in Letcher, County Sanborn, township of Perry in S.D., six miles northeast of Loomis. The McCue's owned a six-room farmhouse on 240 acres just one mile from the local school and attended worship services at the Union Sunday School. In August of 1917 Miss Anderson from the CAS paid a visit and at which time she went to live at the residents of Sherman Lewis who also lived in Letcher, S.D.

Violet is found in the 1920's census records as living in the household of Sarah Anderson, a 68-year-old widow. Mrs. Anderson's 4 grown children are living with her and are proprietors of the local Ice Company. The three boys, John 35, Joseph 33, Charles 30, and the daughter Rea Lewis 24 (the bookkeeper) plus two grandchildren, William 3, and Marie 1 ½. Rea is also Widowed. Violet is working as their housekeeper.

At the age of 58 years old Violet marries Orvis Medworth in Lincoln, S.D. on June 10, 1959. They resided in Mitchell, Davison County, S.D. Orvis died August 9, 1971, Violet passes on July 21, 1984, they are both buried in the Graceland Cemetery, Mitchell S.D.

Arland and Una were placed together as indicated by the Sioux Falls newspaper with Mrs. A.C. Johnson. The Johnson's live in Canton, Lincoln County, S.D.

Arland was born 1903, at the age of twenty-one is living in Pierre, Hughes County, S.D., working as a laborer. He is found in the 1930 census living in Seattle, Washington. He marries first Ella M. Paske, a stenographer, of King, Washington on April 30, 1930. He worked as a hospital attendant in Seattle in his early years before becoming a pipefitter. Arland then marries Margaret (Davis) McMully on January 7th, 1976, they reside in Thurston, Washington. An interesting note found on both of his marriage licenses, Arland's name is Albermond Arland Johnson, it's confirmed that it's Arland, as his parents are listed as Otis Kinney and Lettie Elwood both of Gouverneur, N.Y.

Una, actually was named Unabelle, had moved back to Gouverneur, N.Y. by 1926. She married Everett Given on October 13th. The wedding was held at the First Methodist church at 4:30 in the afternoon. The ceremony was performed by the Rev. Maynard Bearch. Her husband worked as a cheesemaker in Edwards where they reside. Miss Eva Kinney, sister of the bride, was the maid of honor.

Una was living on Pine Street in Potsdam when she died on January 1st, 1984, she died in the Canton-Potsdam hospital. She was survived by two children, a son, Gordon, and Daughter Gloria VanAtter. Also surviving is her sister Violet Medworth of Mitchell, S.D. The obituary lists all of her brothers deceased.

Eva Kinney, the only reference to Eva being a sister in this family is at Una's wedding. Perhaps she was the child that was in the home for "feeble minded children" or an older sibling that wasn't living in the home at the time the earlier census was taken listing the children. The other possibility is that she is Violet M. Kinney, and the reporter got the first name wrong in the wedding announcement.

The Courier & Freeman newspaper of Potsdam, N.Y. dated Tuesday, June 29th, 1976, announced a reunion of the Kinney children after 52 years. Unabelle Davis of Potsdam, Bryan Kinney of Spragueville, Arland, Johnson of Lucey, Washington, Violet Medworth of Mitchell, South Dakota, along with multiple nieces and nephews. The family was separated in 1913 when the youngest three parted on the "Orphan Train", but they stayed connected and three "Orphan Train" riders returned to St. Lawrence County, N.Y. for a family picnic in Potsdam at Unabelle's home.

United Helpers Orphans Home, Ogdensburg, N.Y.

The Havens family:

Mom was Mabel Smith, the daughter of Willard R. and Eva F. Smith. She married first Alfred Smithers, a farmer, on March 10th, 1891, in Heuvelton, N.Y. The ceremony was performed by the Rev. M.W. Chase. Alfred and Mable had one child, a daughter, Ida M., in 1897.

She married a second time, Elmer Havens sometime before 1903. To them were born two children, Charles E., and Marian E.

Mabel died on October 16th, 1908, born in 1874 in Parishville, New York which is located in the east-central part of St. Lawrence County. She's buried in the Pine Hill Cemetery in Oswegatchie, St. Lawrence County. Following mom's death, the three children went to live in Oswegatchie with her parents, Willard R., and Eva F. Smith. Willard worked as a gardener and died October 10th, 1910. Eva was admitted to St. Lawrence Hospital, a.k.a. Ogdensburg State Asylum for the Insane, in 1913

The oldest child, Ida, was sixteen and went to live with relatives in Hermon. At the age of eighteen she married Fay Erwin Peters, age 20, on May 17, 1915. He was the son of Michael and Laura A. (King) Peters.

The younger two children were placed in the "United Helpers Home". This home was formed in about 1898 and was established when ten woman pledged $100 each funding the establishment. The home's purpose was to care for orphaned children and destitute women.

Clara's log indicates their father was "A Drunkard" and had abandoned the children. Their mother was a "Good Woman".

Charles E., case number 8706, and his sister, **Marian E.,** case number 8707, are kept together and are taken in by Sam and Harrietta Thorsen living five blocks northeast of the train depot in Canton, S.D. Arriving on May 8th, 1913. The Thorsens are of the Lutheran faith and have no other children. Mr. Thorson is a retired farmer, owning a ten-room house in town near the school and considered wealthy. Charles's record doesn't indicate any childhood diseases; however, Marian has had measles and chicken pox.

The children are found in the Thorsen household in the 1920 federal census still living in Canton, S.D. At this time Mr.

Thorsen is 58 years old and his wife is fifty-seven. They also have two nephews living with them. Albert Engen aged twenty-eight and his brother Edward aged twenty-five. Both nephews are employed as farmers and were born in Wisconsen.

Ten years later Charles has moved out; however, Marian is living with them with her own daughter. Marian's last name at this time is Rossom. Marian has a daughter at this time, named Doris A. Rossom, born in 1929. Nothing has been found about what happened to Marian's husband that she moved back in with their adopted parents.

Reception

for Orphan Children at the Presbyterian Church

McPherson, Kansas

Friday, December 5, 1924, at 2:00 p. m.

COMMITTEE

W. C. HEASTON, M. D.	F. O. JOHNSON	H. A. ROWLAND
REV. L. H. EAKES	F. A. VANIMAN	RAY STROHM

Chapter 5   Clara's Notes

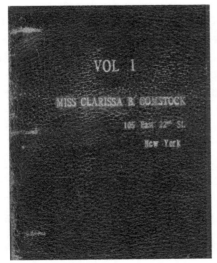

As an agent for the CAS Clara Comstock traveled with her logs (journals). This particular *(pictured)* one was a two-volume set. Names of the "wards" were kept in order by town and/or states where they were placed. Therefore, when she was traveling with a new group of children to one area before returning back to New York City she could visit children placed in various towns throughout the mid-west. As an example, if she was in the region of Afton, Iowa by turning to the Afton section of her log and know which children were in that area for a follow-up visit.

Transcribing notes was straight forward. However, in other cases the dates were hard to follow: An example is **Robert Gudmundsen** listed as born November 39, 1913, picked up from his grandmother's house on February 17, 1913. And placed with a family in Decorah, Iowa on April 1, 1917. One can only assume that the pick-up date is written wrong. And should have been February 13, 1917.

Another example is **Ada Burnham**. Her birth date is listed as March 4, 1916. But she is placed in the home of a **Mr. Gjere** April 24, 1913. All the other children in the section of the book where we find Ada's page have a placement date is 1913. It can only be assumed that the day and year of her birth is also transposed, and she was born March 16, 1904.

This chapter explores the placement of those in Vol. 1 and Vol. 2 of the logs that were made available to the author. The names appear in the order that they are in her journals.

When you see a town name hi-lighted in blue that indicates a new tab in the journal.

Afton, Iowa

Edward Reck, case number 4037, was born July 5, 1897, the son of Edward and Mary (Fransch) Reck. He had been in the Home for Destitute Children (without the basic necessities of life) and had a sister Mimie and brother Nicholas. No information regarding them was found. Remarks read: Mother is Degenerate. He was placed prior to 1910 in Afton, Iowa in the care of G.W. Kelly. March 20, 1918, he joined the U.S.A. Coast Artillery.

Alfred Brogden, case number 4034, was born Dec 9, 1898, to Charles and Mary Brogden an English priest. No information is available regarding the circumstances surrounding him being institutionalized at the B.C.A.S. On March 20, 1918, he was place with U.W. Carter, USA Coast Artillery in Afton, Iowa, two miles south and one mile east of depot.

Algona, Iowa
Committee
H.C. Adams, Real Estate
Dr. M.J. Kenefick, Physician
E.V. Swetting, Lawyer
C.B. Murtagh, Banker
L.J. Dickinson, Lawyer
Frank Henderson, Grocer
Wm. Shirley, Superintendent of Schools

Elmer Barley, case number 10208, was born August 16, 1910.
Leo Barley, case number 10209, was born August 28, 1905. Leo had whooping cough when he was younger.
Their parents were Larenzi and Elizabeth (VanLenvan) Barley. Mom died of heart failure; dad surrendered Elmer and is listed as intemperate.

Elmer was placed on April 6, 1916, with Robert D. Rayster who lives five and a half miles from Algona. He rents 367-acres and lives in an eight-room farmhouse, two miles from the local school.

Leo is placed on April 4, 1916, in the home of Fred A. Will also living in the Algona, Iowa area at RFD #2, three and a half miles northwest of Algona. The Will's family has a six month ond child and are the Methodist faith living in an eight-room farmhouse on 120-acres two miles from the local school.

George W. Bresee, case number 10211, was born January 15, 1902.
Idella Bresee, case number 10212, was born April 15, 1908.
Vesta J. Bresee, case number 10213, was born November 29, 1903, in Middleburgh, N.Y.
Their parents were Martin J. and Effie (Springstead) Bresee. Mr. Bresee worked as a laborer in Steward, N.Y. and following their divorce he surrendered the children to the care of the CAS. Martin is listed as being mentally deficient.

On May 5, 1916, George was placed in the home of Fred L. Zeigler five miles southwest of Algona, Iowa. Residing at RFD #4 the Zeigler's were of the Presbyterian faith. Owns a six-room farmhouse on 160-acres of land.

On May 5, 1916, Idella was placed in the home of George E. Sprangberg, who worked as a mail clerk and was of the Lutheran faith living a mile from Algona at 1024 East McGregor.

Vesta traveled with George and Idella, Vesta went to live with Oscar Anderson at RFD #1 Burt, Iowa eight miles east and two miles south of Algona. The Andersons have a 14-year-old boy and own a farm of 320-acres living in an eight-room farmhouse a mile from the school. They attend the Methodist Episcopal church.

Albert T. Brooks, case number 10527, was born in NYC on June 23, 1907.
Dorothy Brooks, case number 10528, was born in NYC on May 23, 1912.
Their parents were Fred and Elizabeth (Tyler) Brooks. Fred was an upholsterer and when he died the children was surrendered to the CAS by their mother on February 21, 1917. They lived at 220 South 11 Street in Mt. Vernon, N.Y.

On March 17, 1917, Albert went to live with Mrs. E.J. Rawson in Algona, Iowa. The Rawsons were retired and own a ten-room house near the school, they attended the local Baptist church.

Dorothy was placed three days later than her brother Albert on February 24, 1917. She went to live with John Albert Johnson six miles southeast of Algona. Mr. Johnson was of the Congregational faith and lived near the school farming 80-acres of land which they own. The Johnsons had a five-room farmhouse.

Sylvester Eckerson, case number 10215, was born in Schoharie, N.Y. to Charles and Mary (Manchester) Eckerson. There is nothing in the notes that indicate what happened to the parents. Sylvester was picked up by the CAS at the District Attorney of Schoharie County. Sylvester had two sisters, Inas and May. There are no notations on the sisters. George William Godfrey welcomed Sylvester into his home on April 10, 1916. The Godfreys lived three miles east and one mile south at RFT #3, Algona, Iowa. Mr. Godfrey farms his own 160-acres living one and a quarter mile from the school in an eight-room farmhouse and attended the Methodist Episcopal church.

Edward Scheckling, case number 10216, was born in NYC on December 30, 1910. Edward was city number G-13438.
Lena Scheckling, case number 10217, was born in NYC on April 22, 1912. Lena is recorded as city number A-993.
Their parents were Albert and Emma (Kissenbirth) Scheckling and resided on Randall's Island. His mother was declared "mental defective," and the father deserted the family. The children were placed at Five Points House of Industry.

Edward and his sister Lena were kept together and became part of the Frank H. Shockelford family on April 8, 1917. The Shackelford's resided in the town of Algona, Iowa. Mr. Shackelford owns an eight-room townhouse near the school. They were of the Methodist Episcopal faith and his occupation is listed as Harness N. (There is no indication what the "N." stands for.)

Florence Smith, case number 10218, was born February 3, 1906, in Whitenburg, N.Y.
Lillian Smith, case number 10219, was also born in Whitenburg, N.Y. on April 23, 1910.
They were the daughters of Henry and Mable (Taylor) Smith. Florence and her sister Lillian were placed in the Industrial

Home in Kingston, New York on February 8th, 1916. Florence's file documents that she had whooping cough and chicken pox. Their mother's sister was Pearl Taylor and lived in Woodstock, N.Y.

On November 6, 1916, Florence went to live with Edward and Nellie S. Dittmer in Burt, Iowa. Burt is three miles north and two miles east of the depot. The Dittmer's were engaged in farming and lived in an eight-room house on 160-acres. They attended the Methodist Episcopal church and lived three quarters miles from the local school.

Lillian also had the diseases of whooping cough and chicken pox. Her new home was with Herman Dan living at RFD #2 Burt, Iowa. The Dan's lived four miles north of Algona and was engaged in farming, residing on its own160-acres. They attended the Methodist Episcopal church and had one girl and one boy.

Charles Summons, case number 9098, was born January 1902 in Kingston, N.Y. His father was a laborer. Charles was the son of Virgil and Elizabeth Summons. There are no notes on what happened to the parents or why Charles was placed in the Kingston Industrial Home. Charles Johnson took him in on February 5, 1914, and resided at RFD #4 in Ames, Iowa. Ames is four miles southwest of Algona. Mr. Johnson has a 16-year-old boy living with them and owns 105-acres in a seven-room house and is engaged in farming. The local school is one mile from the farm.

Armstrong, Iowa has a notation of a **Viola Schoonmaker** being placed in this town. However, her page had been moved to the Nevada, Iowa section of the book.

Audubon, Iowa
Henry Hastedt, case number 2467, was born October 21, 1901, to Henry B. and Angeline Hastedt. The family resided in Ulster County and also had a girl named Mary Hastedt. Henry was in the Kingston Industrial Home and went to Audubon and taken in by Hanyon Rinemund on June 23, 1903. Mr. Rinemund lived four and a half miles northwest of the depot in an eight-room house on 160-acres. He was engaged in farming,

attended the Methodist Episcopal church, the school was one and a quarter mile from their home.

Avoca, Iowa
Lillian Wallace, case number 2721, was born December 17, 1900, in Bennington, Vt. Her Father was Charles Wallace and Mother Eva LaBarnes. Lillian had a sister Amanda that died. Lillian was turned over to the CAS by her mother. She was placed in the home of C.M. Rife on March 1, 1917, in Avoca, Iowa.

Calmar, Iowa
Maude Schoonmaker, case number 8432, was born April 12, 1905, in Esopus, NY to Charles and Melissa (Smith) Schoonmaker. On November 11, 1912, the poor master of Ulster County sent Maude to the Kingston Industrial School. She had a sister Viola. The mother was in an asylum from injuries received while quarreling with husband. On April 7, 1913, she was placed in the home of Nels N. Kaloos at RFD #3 Calmar, Iowa. They live in a six-room house and own 105-acres engaged in the farming business. Their house is located one and a quarter mile east and three miles west of Calmer and one and a quarter mile from the local school. The family attends the Lutheran church.

Irene Conklin (Travers), case number 8310, was born about 1903 to Eugene and Sarah E. Conklin. Irene was placed with the Overseer of Poor, Westchester County picked up on May 14, 1912. A sister, Rose, was picked up at the same time. The mother was sent to the penitentiary "for keeping a disorderly house." She says her name is Travers. Irene was located in Calo, Iowa at RFD #2 six miles northwest of Fernald with the James Brooks family The Brooks are farmers and own 300-acres one mile from the school. They are of the Methodist faith and have a son aged eighteen. A male servant also lives with them.

Charles City, Iowa
Committee
George T. Heity, Banker
William B. Johnson, Banker
Prof. T. T. Vasey, Superintendent of Schools
Dr. James B. Minner, Physician

E. M. Sherman, Nurseryman
Rev. W. L. Dibble, Con. Minister
J. G. Legel, Druggist & Ex Senator
C. H. Parr, Munition Factory

Charlotte Beatty, case number 10506, was born August 29, 1910, birthplace mentioned as New York State. Her parents, Henry was born in England and Charlotte (Redmond) in Canada. The mother was in the State Hospital for being insane for a brief time. She also had a brother, Edward Guy. Charlotte was put in the care of Jeanette Clay on February 28, 1917, living one mile from Charles City, Iowa. For reasons undocumented she is then moved on March 25, 1917, to the home of Fred M. Lewis of Marble Rock, Iowa. Marble Rock is a half mile from the depot. Mr. Lewis is a farmer who rents 160-acres and owns a seven-room house a half mile from the school and is of the Christian faith.

Evart Watson, case number 10516, was born November 15, 1910, in Russell, N.Y. to William and Ella (Johnson) Watson. They were taken to the United Helpers' Home. Evart had two brothers Glen and Bryon. His grandfather was Andrew Johnson of Russell, N.Y. The father deserted the family of eleven. He was taken in by Earl M. Kemard, P.O. Floyds Crossing, Charles City, Iowa. The family is Methodist Episcopal and has a six-room house and rents 135-acres. Mr. Kemard is engaged in farming and has two daughters aged fifteen and seventeen.

Bertha May Ross, case number 10514, was born March 30, 1906, in Glen Falls, N.Y. to Frank and Minnie (Pease) Ross. Her father, a laborer, deserted the family and mother (immoral) is in the County Home in Warrensburg, N.Y. The CAS workers pick up Bertha from St. Josephs Home on Thompson Street, in Troy, N.Y. On March 1, 1917, she is placed in the home of Niels Peter Clausen of RFD #6 Charles City, Iowa, five miles northeast of the depot. The family is farming a rented 160-acres and lives in a six-room home one and a quarter mile from the school. They are of the Lutheran faith and have an eight-year-old- boy.

William Pierce, case number 10513, was born June 9, 1911, in Gloversville, N.Y.

George Pierce, case number 10512, was also born in Gloversville, N.Y. on May 14, 1906.

Their parents were George and Annie Pierce. George was a mason tender. There are no notes on why William and his brother George were at the M. L. Shaffer Com. Of Charities, Gloversville.

In March of 1917 Dell D. Roberts became the new parent/guardian to William. Mr. Roberts farms his own 80-acres and has nine-room farmhouse two and a half miles from the school. He is of the Methodist Episcopal faith living at RFD #2 Rockford, Iowa. They reside two and a half miles southeast of Rudd, Iowa.

George was taken to Charles City, Iowa six miles southeast of the depot to reside with Frank D. Webster's family on March 1, 1917. His new home is near the school and the Websters own an eight-room house, Mr. Webster is engaged in farming and is of the Methodist Episcopal faith. (The family also took in Gladys Palmer.)

Gladys Palmer, case number 10508, was born in Glen Falls, N.Y. on January 20, 1914.

Ruth Palmer, case number 10509, was born in Glen Falls, N.Y. on November 24, 1915.

They were the children of Albert and Ida (Eckert) Palmer. Albert worked as a laborer and was intemperate while Ida is reported to be immoral with questionable habits. She has three sisters, Stella, Ruth, and Viola. Ida turned the girls over to the Troy Orphan Asylum on January 24, 1917.

On February 28, 1917, Gladys was taken in by Frank D. Webster's family. His new home is near the school and is an eight-room house, Mr. Webster is engaged in farming and is of the Methodist Episcopal faith. (The family also took in George Pierce.)

On March 1, 1917, Ruth begins living with Clifford Gray's family six-blocks northeast of the depot in Charles City, Iowa. Mr. Gray is a grocer living near the school and owns a seven-room home.

Chester, Iowa

Lester Palmer, case number 8337, was born in Greenpoint, Long Island on April 22, 1901.

Howard Palmer, case number 8170, was born November 1897. They are the sons of Lester and Lillian (Priest) Palmer. Lester died and mom is living in Madison Square, Long Island. Lester and his older brother Howard have a married sister, Mrs. Robert Christman who lives at 809 McDonald Street, Brookland, N.Y.

Lester is placed in the home of F. A. Eckstein on August 7th, 1911, located three miles west of the depot. His brother Howard joins the family nine months later. The Eckstein's are farmers living three quarter miles from the local school, living in a ten-room house and are the Methodist Episcopal faith. They own 600-acres of land. When he became of age he joined the Army.

Howard was placed in the New York Juvenile Asylum on April 17, 1912. He is taken in by Mr. Eckstein, the same man that his brother Lester is living with. Everything in the Eckstein family remained the same, however, the farm-acres have been recorded as 500-acres and the farmhouse has twelve-rooms. At this time, it is also noted that Mr. Eckstein has taken on two servants.

Cecil Burnham, case number 8629, was born in England on January 18, 1899, to Harry and Annie Burnham. Harry worked as a laborer, they lived at 523 51st Street, Brooklyn, N.Y. Cecil was taken in by the Five Points House of Industry on April 23, 1913. In November of 1916 Mrs. Sarah Johnson of RFD #1 Chester, Iowa took Cecil to their home, nine miles northeast of the depot. Sarah's husband worked farming. They lived on 83-acres in an eight-room house one and a half mile from the school and were of the Methodist faith. The Johnsons have two children before Cecil came to live with them. On November 28, 1918, Cecil joined the Army.

Chicago, Illinois

John Doane, case number 9532. has no birth or family data available. He was in the Five Points House of Industry, Foundling Asylum. On November 14, 1917, he is placed with

John A. Weber. At 4119 North Monticello Avenue, Chicago. The family lives in five-rooms.

Margaret Kerns, case number 8961, was born to Stella Kerns on July 29, 1900, in Rochester, N.Y. She was placed in the Canandaigua Orphan Asylum in March of 1908. Childhood diseases include whooping cough and measles. Margaret was placed with Reuben Bakewell at RFD #1 Church, Iowa on November 11, 1915. The Bakewells lived thirteen miles northeast of Waukon, Iowa. The family has three boys and lives in an eight-room house on 200-acres. Reuben is engaged in farming, and they are of the Methodist faith. Margaret returns to New York on November 4, 1918.

Clear Lake, Iowa
Harold Backlund, case number 8425, was born in New Jersey to Emil Backlund on September 30, 1906. There is no mention of the mother, he has a brother named George. Harold's city number is A819. On February 7, 1912, he is placed in the Five Points House of Industry by the D.P.C. Harold is taken in by Dr. W. W. Phillips of Clear Lake, Iowa who lives in some "large" rooms at the sanitarium in town.

Stella Palmer, case number 10568, was born March 12, 1912, in Glen Falls, N.Y. to Albert and Ida (Eckert) Palmer. Albert worked as a laborer and was intemperate while Ida is reported to be immoral with questionable habits. There are three more girls in the family, Ruth, Gladys, and Viola. Stella lived with an aunt in Cohoes, N.Y., the aunt found she could no longer keep her. On May 13, 1917, she is taken to Clear Lake, Iowa where she joins the Eugene Grim family who lives three blocks from the depot. The Grim's are of the Methodist Episcopal faith living just four blocks from the school in a ten-room home. Mr. Grim is a wealthy retired farmer.

Alston Hygoard, case number 10507, was born in Canada on March 28, 1904, to Ellis Hygoard, with no mention of his mother. His father was a carpenter who immigrated from Ireland. Ellis has a brother Christopher Hygoard who lives in Selkirk, Manitoba, Canada. Alston was placed in the Brooklyn Orphan Asylum in 1914. He traveled to Charles City, Iowa and joined the James A. Ferguson family on February 28, 1917. Mr. Ferguson owns a home at 201 Eight Avenue near the school in an eight-room house in the city. He was employed by the Hart Parr Company. Then on July 20, 1917, he was taken to Calo, Iowa two and a half miles southwest and resided with David Brooks. Mr. Brooks worked as a farmer and resided in a seven-room house, he has four other children, ages 1, 4, 3, and 7.

Coon Rapids, Iowa

Charles Gartland, case number 2900, was born February 26, 1902, to John and Lizzie (Bannon) Gartland. His father John was indicated as Protestant faith and from Florida, his mother Lizzie was born in New York and is of the Catholic faith. Mom surrendered Charles, as the father has been committed to Sing Sing. On June 14, 1904, he is put in the care of John C. Hooker in Coon Rapids, Iowa four miles south and four miles west of the depot. John Hooker resides in a moderate home farming 80-acres. The school is one and a half miles from where they reside.

Julius Smith, case number 2884, was born in Brooklyn in 1900 to Joseph and Kate (Mulasky) Smith. Julius is listed as city number 510 and is taken to the Eastern District Ind Com. On May 2, 1902. He was placed in the care of A. C. Taylor on June 14, 1904, in Coon Rapids, Iowa. Mr. Taylor is a merchant running the local hardware store. They live near the school and attend the Methodist Church.

Corydon, Iowa

Daniel George, case number 2292, was born March 10, 1899, to Daniel and Christina (Ebruger) George. Mom surrendered Daniel on March 29, 1902, as the father deserted the family. There were two other children, George and Margaret surrendered on February 20, 1902. (Note: the file says the brother's name was George, if that's true his name would have been George George.) Daniel travels to Corydon, Iowa where he will live with Henry J. Haner six miles east of the depot, they reside on 25-acres.

Decorah, Iowa
Committee
February 11, 1913 – April 1, 1913
C. J. Weiser, Banker
Rev. Paul Koran, pastor
Ben Bear
H.J. Green
E.C. Bailey
H.C. Hyerleid

Winnifred Dorothea Austin, case number 8694. Is unique from the other cases. She was born in Decorah, Iowa on March 13, 1913. Austin was her mother's last name. She was picked up from the Reverand Otto Schmidt of Decorah. Winnifred was taken in by H. G. Landmeyer and adopted. They lived seven miles northeast of Decorah and were of the Lutheran faith living one and a half miles from the school on 75-acres in a six-room house. Mr. Landmeyer was engaged in farming.

Edward Dickman, case number 8554, was born December 24, 1901.
William Dickman, case number 8556, was born September 11, 1900.
The boys were the sons of William Dickman. Mr. Dickman was a boiler-maker from Sweden. There is no mention of who his mother was. Edward and his brother William were placed in the Juvenile Asylum on January 28, 1913. Edward's city number was 765 and has two brothers John and William along with a sister Edith of Woodbury, Long Island. Their uncle, Mr. Sandberg, lives at 433 West 117th Street, N.Y.C.

D.C. Hildohl first took in Edward on February 11, 1913, Mr. Hildohl, lived six miles south of Decorah, Iowa at RFD #2. The family had a large house farming 120-acres one mile from the school. They were of the Lutheran faith and had three girls. On November 15, 1914, Edward was then taken in by H. Meyron who also lived in the Decorah, Iowa area.

William was placed in the home of Paul E. Egge residing at RFD #1 Decorah, Iowa located six miles south-east of the depot. Mr. Egge also had a large house farming 200-acres. The family had two girls and lived one and a quarter mile from the local school and was of the Lutheran faith.

Ada Burnham, case number 8628, was born in England on March 4, 1916. She's the daughter of Harry and Annie Burnham, Harry worked as a laborer. There is no mention of what happened to the father; however, mom resides at 523 51st Street Brooklyn. In April 1913 she is placed in Spring Grove, Minnesota at RFD #4 nine miles south of Spring Grove and fifteen miles north of Decorah, Iowa. N.A. Gjere takes her into their home, which is an eight-room farmhouse. Mr. Gjere farms 65-acres three quarter miles from the local school and is of the Lutheran faith.

Winnifred Galusha, case number 8631, has no birthdate listed. Her father, a laborer, is Walter Galusha with no mention of a mother. Winnifred was picked up by the Overseer of Poor, Edward Griggs in Warrensburg, N.Y. in March of 1913. Mrs. Elene Hanson takes her in on March 8, 1913. Mrs. Hanson, a Lutheran, lives on the west side in Decorah, Iowa at 803 Mound Street in an eight-room townhome one mile from the local school.

Robert Gudmundsen, case number 8632, was born on November 29, 1913.
Walter Gudmundsen, case number 8633, was born in N.Y.C. on December 8, 1902.
They were the sons of Guston and Lydia (Nicholson) Gudmundsen. Guston worked as a bartender. After Lydia died, the children were sent to their grandmother, Mrs. Catherine Nicholson who resided at 178 East 117th Street, N.Y.C. The CAS picked Robert and his brother Walter up from the grandmother.

Robert was placed in the home of E.F. Bakken on April 1, 1913, who resides at RFD #5, five miles west of Decorah, Iowa. Mr. Bakken, a Lutheran farmer, has a ten-room house on 240-acres across the road from the school.

Walter first joined the household of B.O. Bakken on April 1, 1913, at RFD #5 six miles west of Decorah, Iowa. The Badden family is of the Lutheran faith living in a ten-room house, farming

400-acres. They live one mile from the local school. He is actually one mile from his brother and attending the same school. The two Bakken's are from the same families, and the brothers see each other during family visits. There is no date associated but Walter was moved to the household of August Schwartz in Eagle, Wisconsin RFD #1.

Nelson Maxim, case number 8634, was born on May 5, 1904 to James Mixon and Alice Combs. James worked as a laborer and Alice is listed as "older" living in Warrensburg, N.Y. He is listed as joining the J.J. Hugas family on April 1, 1913, in Dorchester, Iowa, ten miles south of Spring Grove. The Hugas are Lutherans living a half mile from the school in an eight-room house farming his own 60-acres. His mother surrendered him to the Troy Orphan Asylum.

Fred Older, case number 8635, was born in Warrensburg, N.Y. on May 5, 1907, to Edward and Alice (Combs) Older. Edward worked as a laborer and they lived in Horicon, N.Y. (He is a half-brother to Nelson Maxim, he had a brother James Older, no information is available on James.) His bother surrendered him to the Troy Orphan Asylum. He went to live in the suburbs of Decorah, Iowa with Nels O. Ashem on April 2, 1913. Mr. Ashem has a small farm, works as a milkman, and lives in a six-room home. They attend the Lutheran church.

Joseph Miller, case number 8562. Was born to Joseph and Ellen (Alapa) Miller on May 8, 1906. Joseph worked as a Hotel Keeper and deserted the family, moving to Vermont. Joseph has three sisters, Ruby, Ellen, and Violet along with three brothers, Balden, Raymond, and Frank. He was staying at the Mohawk & Hudson River Humane Society before being taken in by John Ballinger of Decorah, Iowa on February 19, 1913. Mr. Ballinger was the town butcher living in a ten-room house.

Leona Philo, case number 8636, was born in Glen Falls, N.Y. on December 8, 1901. Her parents are Frank and Eleanor (VanLein) Philo and lives in Glen Falls. Frank worked as a laborer and surrendered Leona to the Albany Orphan Asylum. On April 4, 1913, Nels E. Ramsey takes her in, residing at RFD #1, five miles southeast of Decorah, Iowa. The Ramsey family attend the Lutheran church living a half mile from the local school in a ten-room house and owns 160-acres. There are two children in their family, a boy and a girl.

Harold Krauss, case number 8558, was born December 24, 1900, in Brooklyn, N.Y. Harold is city number A367.
Mildred Krauss, case number 8560, was born March 12, 1904. Mildred is city number A-369.
The family was of the Protestant faith. They were born to William and Annie E. (Cummings) Krauss and resided in Brooklyn. They have a sister, Mable, and were placed in the E.D.I.S. on November 2, 1908, by D.P.C.   Their grandmother, Mrs. Mary Krauss, residing at 1172 Green Avenue, Brooklyn. An uncle John Krauss who resided at 1482 Kalb Avenue, Brooklyn.
Harold was placed on February 11, 1913, in the home of Frank Pilgrim who resided six miles west of Decorah took in all three children. Frank lived one and a half mile from the school and farmed 160-acres.   (Mable; however, was pulled out of this home and replaced, see Mable's entry.)

Their sister Mable was also placed in this household, but for some reason was pulled out of this home on April 3, 1913. (See her records.)

DeFiance, Iowa
William Joseph Brooks, case number 2893, was born in N.Y.C. on October 3, 1899.
Alfred Brooks, case number 2894, was born in N.Y.C. on November 28, 1902.
Their parents were Fred and Elizabeth (Tyler) Brooks. Fred is from San Francisco and works as an upholsterer while mom came from New Jersey and is of the Presbyterian faith. There are six children in the household, mom gives up William and his brother Alfred to the CAS as she states she can't provide for these two.

On June 14, 1904 both brothers are taken on the train to Iowa. William is placed in the care of Andy Allen two and a half miles northwest of Mapleton, Iowa. Mr. Allen farms 240-acres one-and three-quarter miles from the local school. He has four children ages 3 mo., 12 and 16. On October 23, 1904, William is then moved to the home of A.R. Tryon of Defiance, Iowa, two and a half mile southwest of the depot. When William became of age he joined the Army.

Alfred was placed in the care of Mrs. William Holmes one and a half miles south of Defiance. The Holmes are of the Christian faith, living near the school in a large home. Mr. Holmes works as a carpenter.

DeWitt, Iowa

Jesse Reynolds, case number 3820, was born in January of 1902. His father (also named) Jesse worked as a laborer. There is no mention of the mother's name. He was picked up by the CAS from Commissioner Noyes in Gloversville, N.Y. He also has a brother named George and a grandfather, David Reynolds of Edinburgh, N.Y. Jesse joined the Gus Grimm family on January 2, 1906, five miles northwest of DeWitt, Iowa residing at RFD #5.

Fred Hayden, case number 3814, was born January 28, 1900, in N.Y.C. to William and Fannie Hayden and was the ward of the city and placed in the Nursery and Childs Hospital. Fred has two brothers, George and Homer. On January 2, 1906, he was in the care of Jake McCarl residing in the town of DeWhitt, Iowa. When he became of age he joined the Navy.

DuBuque, Iowa

Janette Reed, case number 9042, was born on June 27, 1900, to Chester and Helena (King) Reed. Her father deserted her and the mother's whereabouts are unknown. The only notes indicate that Janette was taken to the "House of Good Shephard" in DuBuque, Iowa.

Dunlap, Iowa

Waldemere Rosin, case number 8320, was born in N.Y.C. on February 4, 1905, to Guster and Theresa Rosin. Guster lived at 901 East 135th Street in N.Y.C. and was a native of Sweden. Waldemere was turned over to the Nursery and Child's Hospital, listed as city number 6084 and had had whooping cough and measles. There is no date of when he went to live with H.W. Hodkins of RFD #5 seven miles northwest of Dunlap, Iowa. Mr. Hodkins owns a 160-acre farm, living in an eight-room house just a half mile from the local school.

Estherville, Iowa
Committee
B.B. Anderson, Mayor
W.W. Walker, Banker
A. Patcher, Real Estate
Henry Mahlum, Furniture
G. Zeeman, Banker
Carl Geglum, Merchant

Russell Hampstead, case number 9500, has no birthdate listed. He is the son of Harvey and Gertrude Hempstead. Harvey worked as a laborer and Gertrude as a servant. The Hampsteads are from Cairo, Greene County, N.Y. and separated. On October 23, 1914, Russell was taken in by J.W. Fisher, a restaurant owner who owns a seven-room home in the town of Wallingford, Iowa.

Jean Hewitt, case number 9502, has no information regarding her birthdate or parents. She was brought to the office of the Nursery and Child's Hospital, on December 12, 1912, by Mrs. Reeser of 184 Rivington Street, N.Y.C. who found the child on her premises on December 11, 1912, at 8:30 a.m. G.W. Swanson took in Jean, Swanson's live five miles southwest of Estherville at RFD #2. In May of 1917 there were inquiries about adoption.

Mabel Lamphear, case number 8761, was born September 2, 1907, at Yaphank, Long Island. Her mother was fifteen when she was born, her name is listed as Marie Liebhertz and father only as Jones. Mabel was surrendered by Mrs. A.M. Lamphear who resides at 215 West 100th Street in N.Y.C. and has had the child for four years. On October 28, 1914, Dr. M.E. Wilson of Estherville, Iowa took her in. The doctor was of the Presbyterian faith and lived just three blocks from the local school in an eight-room house in town.

Willie Wiggens, case number 9505, was born February 22, 1909, the only thing known about him is he is a foundling (an abandoned infant discovered and cared for by others). Willie was put in the care of W.A. Corkle of RFD, Dolliver, Iowa two and a half miles north of Estherville's depot. Mr. Corkle owns a farm of 160-acres and resides in a seven-room home.

Edwood, Iowa

Harold Grother, case number 2892, was born January 30, 1899, to Eugene and Jennie Grother. Eugene is of German descent and there is no indication to what happened to the parents. Harold's city number is 935. June 14th 904 he was place in care of D.L. Newman who lists as farms, residing in a large home near the school and attends the Presbyterian church. The Newmans live in the town of Mapleton and have three girls. In November of 1905, Harold is in the care of Mrs. Ida Smith, a widow who lives five blocks from the depot in Edgewood, Iowa, and lives near the school.

Jeanette Benham, case number 6359, was born November 23, 1899, in Summersville, Mass. Her parents are Archibold S. and Annie (Kelly) Benham. Archibold was born in New England and Annie was born in Toronto, Ontario, Canada. Jeanette was admitted to the Southern Tier Orphans Home in Elmira, N.Y. on March 14, 1907. She had two brothers Archie and John; on whom there is no file in Miss Comstock's book. On September 15, 1909, she departed Elmira on the train west. Jeanette was moved over an eight-year period into nine various homes.

She went first to live with the Rev. Francis M. DeWeese on September 21, 1909, in Plainview, Nebraska, living in the town. The Reverend lived in the parsonage near the school and preached at the Presbyterian church.

June 30, 1910, she then joined the J.H. Boyce household in Pierce, Nebraska. Mr. Boyce worked as a painter and lived near the school.

September 10, 1910, she rejoins the Reverend DeWeese and his family but this time living at 3223 Gilpin Street, Colo, Denver Township, Iowa. In Colo, the minister is again preaching at the presbyterian church and living in the parsonage.

On May 3, 1912, Joseph Houch takes her in, he lives ten miles northwest of Corning, Iowa. Mr. Houch farms 200-acres and lives a half mile from the local school. He has one grown child.

Next in September of 1912 W.J. Hill has her joining his household in Corning, Iowa. Mr. Hill works as a farmer, and they live near the school with two other children in the household.

March 30, 1915, she goes to live with Albert A. Brehamer at 703 Hickory Street in Atlantic, Iowa. No other information was noted in her file about the Brehamer family.

Just two weeks later on April 13, 1915, she then goes to live with H.P. Thede four miles northwest of Durant, Iowa at RFD #1. The Thede family are of the Presbyterian faith living on 160-acres, one and a quarter mile from the local school and has three children.

She is found placed just 2 days before her 17th birthday, on November 21, 1916, in the care of Miss Josepha Roberts, a supervisor of the local hospital. Miss Roberts is of the Presbyterian faith.

An additional note on the back of her page in Miss Comstock's book reads; "Also visited August 23, 1917, now in Franklin, Nebraska attending school at the Franklin Academy."

Fayette, Iowa
Committee
J. Babcock
O. Stevenson
Emil Hartman
John Graf
Chas Carpenter
M. Humphrey

Vera Burnham, case number 8630, was born on February 9, 1903, in England to Harry and Annie Burnham. She was the ward of the city and placed at the Five Points House of Industry. She went to live with the family of John Langerman in Fayette, Iowa Three and a half miles southeast of the town. Mr. Langerman was of the Methodist faith living on 120-acres, the house had eight-rooms, one and a half miles from the school.

Arthur Clark, case number 8165, was born to Arthur and Florence (Disburger) Clark. The files have no mention of his actual birthdate. Arthur was placed in the E.D.I.S.A. on April 24, 1912. His father is listed as being 25 years old and mother died, he had no known relatives. On May 1, 1912, Arthur was placed in the care of Charles Carpenter, a banker, living in the town of Fayette, Iowa near the school. Mr. Carpenter was of the Methodist Episcopal faith.

Josephine Eberhardt, case number 8161, no birthdate listed nor are the parents listed.
Alice Eberhardt, case number 8160, was born April 15, 1905.
Pearl Eberhardt, case number 8162, has no birthdate listed.
The three girls were in the custody of the Superintendent of the Poor in Saratoga County, N.Y. The father had died, and mother lived in Niskayuna, N.Y.

Josphine was placed with Ed Page in Madena, Iowa who is farming 160-acres. The Page family live in eight-room house two miles from the local school and three miles from the school. They have three other children in the household.

Alice was put in the care of Jesse Holtzman on May 1, 1912. The Holtzmans lived two miles southwest of Lima and three miles northeast of Fayette at RFD #4 Fayette, Iowa. The home consists of seven-rooms on 150-acres. They are farmers who attend the Methodist Episcopal Church and live three quarter miles from the local school. Ther is a boy in the family.

Pearl went to live with James Hutchinson's family on May 1, 1912. The Hutchinson's are farming 280-acres, living in a seven-room house one and a half mile from school. There are two boys in the household, and they are of the Protestant faith. The farm is located four miles north of Fayette, Iowa living at RFD #4.

William Hyieges, case number 8167, was born September 20, 1903. His father is listed as August Rasmussen, Mother Julia. William's city number is A464 and was placed in the Five Point House of Industry. The mother deserted him, and his father is living in Ossining. On May 1, 1912, he is put in the care of W.W. Alley who lives five miles northwest of Fayette at RFD #4 Hawkeye, Iowa.

Estelle McDowell, case number 8168, was born November 26, 1905.

John McDowell, case number 8169, was born August 28, 1899 Their parents were William and Charlotte McDowell. She has a brother, John, and they were picked up from their cousin's, Mrs. Jennie McNamara. On May 1, 1912, the children both went into the care of Forest Johnson two miles north of Fayette, Iowa living at RFD #6. Mr. Johnson owns a farm consisting of 200-acres near the school and they live in six-room house three miles from the local church.

Forest City, Iowa
Committee
Eugene Secor
Dr. H.R. Irish
O. Albert Olson
Dr. J.H. McKay
Ray Jacobs
B.A. Plummer
Dr. Martin Heglund

Agnes Herlin, case number 10724, was born August 25, 1912, to Anthon Anderson and Ovidia Herlin. Her father was from Norway, and she has a sister Evelyn. The CAS picked her up from the Brooklyn Nursery and Infant Hospital on 396 Herkimer Street. On October 12, 1917, Agnes was placed in the care of T.E. Jenson of who lived in the town of Forest City, Iowa. The Jenson's were of the Lutheran faith living near the school. Mr. Jenson worked as a wagon maker, owned a-lot with a nine-room house on it and had two boys ages 9 and 12.

Harry Fleming, case number 10723, was born to George Flemings on April 30, 1910. Moms only has here last name of Hughes is listed as dead. Dad worked as a laborer in the Coal Yards of Beacon, N.Y., and deserted him at the State Charities Aid Association. Harry had childhood diseases of Measles, chicken pox and mumps. His grandmother is Mrs. Delia Pyres Daison. There were two other children, George and Agnes. Harry went to live with August Winkleman on October 12, 1917, one mile south and three miles east of Buffalo Center, Iowa. Mr. Winkleman works his own 640-acres. The lived in an eight-room house and attended the Baptist church. There were six other children in the family.

Forest Moore, case number 10726, was born November 14, 1908.
Violet Moore, case number 10728, was born January 11, 1911.
Helen Moore, case number 10727, was born January 2, 1907.
Their parents were Claude and Louse (Pulver) Moore. Claude is listed as a farm hand and is intemperate. Louise is immoral and feeble minded. The children were placed with the Board of Child Welfare in Dutchess County, N.Y.

Forest and Violet are placed together in the home of Alber Soals on October 12, 1917. The family lives two- and three-quarter miles from the depot in Forest City, Iowa in a seven-room house, Mr. Soals farms own120-acres. They resided three quarter miles from the local school.

On October 12, 1917, Helen is placed in the care of Frank Russell in the town of Forest City, Iowa. Mr. Russell retired is wealthy and lives in a nine-room house near the school and attends the Methodist Episcopal church.

Percy Seymour, case number 10729, was born February 10, 1913, to Clarence and Myrtle (Martin) Seymour. Clarence died; he had worked as a laborer. Myrtle is listed as immoral and Percy was put in the Southern Tier Orphan Asylum in Elmira, N.Y. Percy is taken into the home of Louis Barth who resides a half mile south and six and a half miles east of Forest City, Iowa. The Presbyterian church is four miles from their home and the school is one and a quarter mile. Mr. Barth works farming his own120-acres and resides in an eight-room home.

Edward Wixon, case number 10732, was born on October 5, 1916, to Edward and Beatrice May Wixon. Edward was an illegitimate child turned over by his mother. He was taken to RFD #2 Forest City, Iowa one mile west and a half mile north of Lelan, Iowa to live with Henry Schultz's family. Mr. Schultz worked farming a rented 160-acre, living in a seven-room house one mile from the school. They were of the Methodist Episcopal faith and had a five-year-old girl.

James Fred Williams, case number 10731, was born on August 1, 1914. His mother's maiden name was Martin. He was staying at Sheltering Home Inc., in Geneva, N.Y. He was taken in by Earl William Smith on October 12, 1917. Mr. Smith lives on a rented 160-acre farm in a seven-room house. They reside at RFD #3 four miles northwest of Forest City, Iowa. The school is one and a quarter mile from their home and they attend the Methodist Episcopal church.

Grand Mound, Iowa

Gustave Lundberg, case number 2222, was born in N.Y.C. on May 18, 1899. His parents were Frederick and Christina (Rosen) Lundberg.   Frederick worked as an Iron Worker and had abandoned the family.   Christina died of consumption since May 22, 1902, when she surrendered two older boys George and Lawrence.   The CAS received Gustave from his sister, Bertha, whom he had been living with since December 16, 1902.   On October 26, 1916, Gustave went to live with Alfed Reimer north of Grand Mound, Iowa. They lived in an eight-room farmhouse on 160-acres, one mile from the local school. He went to fight in WW I, died on July 22, 1918.

Greenfield, Iowa

Clarence Ruhl, case number 5693, was born on March 5, 1900. His parents both born in Germany and of the protestant faith were Laurence and Dorothy Carpenter. Clarence was living with his sister prior to July 14, 1908, at 449 West 40 Street, N.Y.C. She married Mr. A.B. Lannamann and moved to 562 West 164 Street. From there on December 27, 1912, the sister moves to Jewett City, Connecticut before moving on June 16, 1916, back into the city to reside at 500 West 176 Street.   F.W. Albrecht took Clarence in on September 8, 1908, eight and a half miles southeast of Cambridge, Nebraska. On April 23, 1909, he then goes to reside with B.S. Resseque, six miles southeast of Cambridge. Then on January 18, 1910, he is in the care of N.A. Wright residing eight miles southeast of Irvin, Iowa. And on May 28, 1912, Mr. Wright moved seven miles northeast of Greenfield, Iowa.

Rose Conklin, case number 8366, has no date of birth listed. Mother, Sarah Conklin, is in prison and the father, Eugene, is living in Peekskill, N.Y. Miss J. Long, state agent for Westchester

County, received Rose from her father. Rose is put in the care of Mrs. Alixander McKay living six miles northeast of Harmony, Minnesota at RFD #1.

Wallace Dunn, case number 6264, was born March 13, 1905. Miss Comstock's notes simply say he was deserted by his father. The Superintendent of Poor for Saratoga County had custody before being taken care of by Fred G. Beck on July 6, 1909, who lived twelve miles east of Greenfield, Iowa in Hebron. Mr. Beck farmed for others and lived one mile from the local school and was of the Protestant faith. Wallace was then put in the care of Chris Hoaf on October 18, 1909, who farms 200-acres that he rents and lives 40-rods from the local school. The Hoafs are of the Methodist Episcopal Faith.

Hepburn, Iowa

Francis Anderson, case number 9496, was born in Norway on June 29, 1906. Both of his parents are listed as deserted. They were Frank and Lizzie Anderson. Francis was placed with the Church Charity foundation. In December of 1915 Simeon Applequest took Francis into his household seven miles southwest of Hepburn, Iowa. Mr. Applequest lives in a five-room house and works as a farmer on property rented from his father. The local school is one mile away and they attend the Lutheran church.

Henry Koedel, case number 7757, was born in N.Y.C. on January 1, 1999, to Anton and Josephine (Imelowitz) Koedel. Anton was born in Germany and worked as a waiter. Josephine was born in Hungary. Henry was at the Five Point House of Industry in N.Y.C. before joining the Simeon Applequest household on September 20, 1911. (See Francis Anderson for details about the Applequests')

Percy Barley, case number 10210, was born in Olive, N.Y. on October 12, 1908. Lorenzo and Elizabeth (VanLenvan) Barley were his parents. Lorenzo worked as a laborer; Elizabeth is listed as dead. Lorenzo surrendered Percy to the Kingston Industrial Home. Whooping cough is listed as a childhood disease, and he is put into the care of Claude L. Sanders on September 14, 1916. Mr. Sanders lived six miles northeast of Ames, Iowa and ten miles northwest of Nevado, Iowa in Ames,

Iowa. The Sanders rents a seven-room house on 240-acres just a quarter mile from the local school. On March 20, 1918, he is placed in the care of N.A. Wright who lives ten miles east of Greenfield, Iowa on 160-acres. Then on August 22, 1918, he joins the Simeon Applequest. (See Francis Anderson for details about the Applequests')

Hopkinton, Iowa
Alfred Bowman, case number 3994. This case the dates must have an error in one of them; my guess would be the year of birth. Alfred is listed as being born on February 4, 1886, and put in the Sheltering Arms Nursery Home on March 12, 1906. Therefore, going to a Nursery in 1906 leads one to believe he was born in 1906. He was born to Tony Bauman and Eliza Ulshoefen. Tony, aged sixty-seven, is the grandfather of Eliza, age 23. Alfred is placed in the home of Mat Pierce on March 13, 1917. Mr. Pierce lives in the town of Hopkinton, Iowa. If born in 1906 would make him 11 years old.

Joseph Rowland, case number 3989, was born February 17, 1903, to George and Sadie (Rowan) Rowland. He has a brother named Ira; mom gave him to the CAS when the father deserted the family. Joseph was placed in the care of B.C. Kurth (no date listed) who lives at RFD #1 two miles northeast of Hopkinton, Iowa.

Humbolt, Iowa
Jack Gunnison, case number 8367, was born July 10, 1906. His parents are not known, he is placed on July 10, 1909, by the D.P.C. in the Home of Destitute Children. His city number is A693. On October 2, 1912, Jack is put in the care of William Holt how lives nine miles north of LaPorte City, Iowa at RFD #4. Mr. Holt owns a farm consisting of 380-acres and lives just one mile from the school.

Iowa Falls, Iowa
Chester Partington, case number 8892, there is no information on Chester. He was placed on November 14, 1913, with J.E. Tuttle who resides are Iowa Falls, Iowa. Mr. Tuttle is a Manager of Electric living three-blocks from the school and is of the Lutheran faith and has an eight-room house.

George Heintz, case number 2700, was born in New York on July 24, 1896, to Alexander and Grace Heintz. He was committed to the Five Point House of Industry on January 9, 1899, by D.P.C. The remarks said he was discharged to the society by D.P.C. and he is listed as city number 1856. On January 26, 1904, George is in the care of Charles Goswell at RFD #1 seven miles west of New Sharon in Taintor, Iowa. Mr. Goswell works as a farmer and resides in a large house three quarters of a mile from the school. On a visit dated June 9, 1916, he is listed with an occupation of Farm work and had finished the eighth grade and attending the methodist church.

Henry Dichting, case number 2707, was born in Brooklyn, N.Y. on July 3, 1897. His parents were Edmand and Mary (Fuller) Dichting. Henry was city number 302 and placed in the Eastern District Industry Home. On January 26, 1904, he is placed in the care of Thomas E. Goswell living seven and a half miles south of New Sharon at RFD #1 Janitor, Iowa. On June 9, 1916, CAS worker Miss Anderson visited. At this time, the Goswell family had moved and are living four miles southwest of New Sharon, Iowa. Mr. Goswell is working a 90-acre farm, they attend the Methodist church and live one and a half miles from the school. However, Henry has finished the eighth grade, and his occupation is also listed as Farming.

Lansing, Iowa
Committee
Mr. Thomas, Banker
Rev. Kegel, Methodist Minister

Arthur Cruys, case number 10378, was born in Hoboken, N.Y. on May 14, 1904, to Herman Cruys, a basket maker. No other information is available on Arthur's background. He was placed in the care of Henry Olson; the date wasn't recorded. Mr. Olsen lives nine miles northwest of Harpers Ferry, Iowa at RFD #1. The Olson family owns an eight-room house farming 160-acres. They are of the Lutheran faith, have three boys and live one and a half miles from the local school. In 1917 Arthur is attending the sixth grade.

Harold Freeman, case number 9093, was born on November 29, 1897. On February 3, 1914, he is placed in the care of Thorwald Halverson, a farmer, living four miles west of Lansing, Iowa. The only other notation on this record indicates in 1917 he had "aged out" of the system.

Edward Heyer, case number 8614, was born on May 12, 1899, in Kings Park, Long Island. His parents were Emile and Ceclia Heyer. Emile was a contactor and of the Protestant faith; while Cecila was of the Catholic faith and died three and a half years prior to his father turning him over to the CAS workers on February 11, 1913. Emile lived at 1238 Atlantic Avenue, Brooklyn, N.Y. Edward was placed in the home of Carl Halverson in Lancing, Iowa. The family lived in a six-room house, farming 200-acres.

Mary Jackson, case number 9039, was born in Brooklyn on August 6, 1903. Both her parents James and Mary Wanda Jackson were both natives of Brooklyn. The CAS picked her up from the Ottilie Orphan Asylum and she was taken in by Howard Woodmansee on January 17, 1904. Her new home was eleven miles south of Uankon, Iowa at RFD #2 Monona, Iowa. The Woodmansee's lived on his own 80-acres. On June 18, 1917, Mary was put in the care of John Huffman who resided at RFD #2 Waterville, Iowa. Mr. Huffman worked farming, owned a six-room house, and lived one and a half miles from the local school. He had two grown children, a boy aged twenty-six and a girl aged nineteen. Then on August 4, 1917, Mary is moved to Mena Bechtel's home at One West Main Street in Lancing, Iowa. Mena is retired and owns an eight-room house, The Bechtel's had one child, a 41-year-old son.

Robert LeRoy, case number 10725, has no personal data listed. He was put in the care of Bernhart Peterson on October 12, 1917. The Peterson's resided at RFD #1 Blooming Prairie, Minnesota. The directions read that they live either seven miles south or five miles north of Lansing. Mr. Peterson is farming his own 140-acre their farmhouse had seven-rooms, one and a half miles from the local school and is a Lutheran. On October 26, 1917, there is a notation that Robert is in the second grade.

Gertrude Perry, case number 3996, was born September 24, at Deans Carnes, N.Y. Her birth year is assumed to be 1901. Gertrude's parents are Fred J. and Laura Perry. The CAS picks her up at the Albany Orphan Asylum. Notes for March 13, 1906, only indicate she's living at RFD, eight miles from Lancing Iowa. There is no indication of who she is living with. A second notation simply says on October 6, 1912, she is living with O.W. Johnson.

Leon Edward Reynolds, case number 9799, was born on October 3, 1911, in Messena, N.Y. The parents' notes read: Frank Reynolds, Almo House. Elizabeth Kirkey, Chases Mills. Leon was surrendered to the United Helpers Home by the Oversee of Poor from Messena, N.Y. On April 23, 1915, he is taken in by Albert Christianson of RFD #2, seven-miles west of Lansing, Iowa. The home is an eight-room house on his own190-acre farm. The family is Lutheran and lives a half mile from the local school.

Lulu Veritzan, case number 8799, was born August 1, 1901, in Brooklyn to Oscar and Annie (Smith) Veritzan. The CAS workers picked her up from the Orphan Asylum Society. There is no date listed of when Mrs. M.E. Feurhelm took her into their household. Her new home is located seven and a half miles west of Church, Iowa at RFD #1. They own a farm of 240-acres and reside in an eight-room house a half mile from the school and attend the Methodist Episcopal church.

Howard Vreeland, case number 10873, was born January 6, 1906, in N.Y. State.
Kenneth Vreeland, case number 10874. Was born in N.Y. State on December 25, 1904.
The sons of John and Ida (Miller) Vreeland. John worked as a laborer, nothing else is known about either parent. They have another brother, LeRoy.

Howard had Measles as a child and was at the Susan F. Cooper Foundation Home, Cooperstown, N.Y. LeRoy is in the care of William A. Hand of Cooperstown. On May 13, 1919, Howard is taken in by Fred Kehr at RFD #1, five miles north of Waterville, Iowa. Mr. Kehr rents a six-room house and is farming 120-acres.

They live a quarter mile from the school and attend the Lutheran church. The Kehrs have two children.

Kenneth had Measles as a child. On May 13, 1918, he went to live with Carl Schafer seven miles southwest of Lansing, Iowa.

LaPorte City, Iowa
Committee
Dr. Fields

Robert MacKenzie Morris, case number 8372, was born on October 29, 1907, in Washington, D.C. to Olive Morris. He had Measles and was taken by the CAS from the *House of Mercy in Washington, D.C.* On October 10, 1912, Robert is taken in by Peter R. Howell, a retired farmer. The Howell owns an eight-room house in the suburbs of LaPorte City, Iowa. The Howell's are of the Methodist Episcopal faith.

note this is the only child that appears in Clara's book that was escorted from a location outside of New York State.

Julia Anna Volkert, case number 8434, was born in Brooklyn on August 11, 1903, to William L. and Margaret (Zeltner) Volkert. They resided at 143 Cooper Street, Brooklyn, N.Y. When Margaret died Julia was surrendered by her father. On October 11, 1917, William M. Holt takes her in, he lives at RFD #4 LaPorte, Iowa, which is four miles southwest of Washburn and nine miles Northwest of LaPorte, Iowa. The Holt's live in a six-room home. They farm their own 80-acres and rent an additional 160-acres one and three quarters miles from the school. They have one boy in the household.

Frank Miller, case number 8270, has no information about him. (See the information on his brother, Joseph Miller.) He was put in the care of James M. Halligan on April 19, 1916, at RFD #3 located four miles south of Letcher, S.D. The Halligans are of the catholic faith, own a five-room home farming 160-acres. The local school is two miles from their home. Notation dated April 19, 1916; indicates he had joined the Army.

Lenox, Iowa

Leonard Wilson, case number 3105, was born June 8, 1902, to Helen M. Wilson. The CAS workers picked him up from The Anchorage in Elmira, N.Y. Leonard was placed on December 6, 1904, in the care of S.E. Wainwright, a wealthy lumberman living in the town of Lenox, Iowa. Their home consisted of twelve-rooms, and they had a son. Leonard attended the local high school.

George Wexler, case number 4546, was born on April 27, 1903, to Aaron and Pearl Wexler. Aaron worked at a newsstand. His Aunt, Mrs. Fannie Emterge turned him over to the CAS. On February 23, 1917, he went to live with Charles Bovee four miles west of Chester Iowa at RFD #2. The Bovees farmed 24-acres and lived one and a half miles from the school in a seven-room house. They are of the Protestant faith and have two girls. On August 1, 1917, he then goes to live with Carl F. Schafer seven miles southwest of Lansing, Iowa. Mr. Shafer is farming 120-acres living in an eight-room home. He too is of the protestant faith and have two girls. They live one mile from the school.

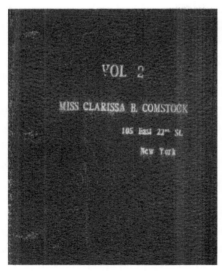

Manchester, Iowa
Committee
Dr. J.J. Lindsley
Calvin Youran
H.L. Rann
William Blake
Burton Clark
A.B. Ferrell

Harry Dishman, case number 8312, was born to Harry and Mary Dishman on February 13, 1908, in N.Y.C. Mr. Dishman worked as a stableman. Harry's city number was 552 and was in the Five Points House of Industry place by D.P.C. On July 17, 1912, he was taken in by Frank Assmus who lived in the town of Manchester, Iowa. Mr. Assmus was a druggist. On August 18, 1912, Miss Rugh Davey became the caregiver, living in the town of Earlville, Iowa. It was three years later, on August 3, 1915, he then went to live with George

G. Davey. George was a gardener living a half mile northeast of Earlville, Iowa, on 120-acres in a seven-room house. He was of the Protestant faith and lived just a half mile from the school. George Davey had two grown children.

George Hasbrouch, case number 8318. There is no information regarding him or any dates. He is in the home of Lester Pilgrim who lived three and a half miles north of Manchester, Iowa.

Esther Holman, case number 7794, was born on February 14, 1906, in Dover, N.H. He is the son of George Carpenter and Margaret Pierce. George was from Main and of the protestant faith. Margaret also of the protestant faith was from New Jersey. Esther was in the care of her grandfather, Robert W. Holman who resided at 1575 St. John's Place in Brooklyn. The notes read: "A small legacy of probably several hundred dollars for Esther is pending in the Brooklyn Surrogate Court, coming from the mother's side, may not be paid until of age." On October 17, 1911, Esther was put in the care of Robert Baster Field who resides one mile east of Scarsdale, N.Y. Mr. Field is an architect who owns an eight-room home and has a three-and-a-half-year-old boy. On December 18, 1911, Rev. G.B. Young took her in residing at 458 3rd Street, N.Y. It was on July 18, 1912, she was then taken west to the home of Anzie Davey who lives five-blocks northeast of Earlville, Iowa. Mr. Davey farms 120 rented-acres and lives four blocks from the local school.

Ellen Miller, case number 8314, is thought to have been born in 1907.
Ruby Miller, case number 8315, was born November 27, 1904.
Violet Miller, case number 8316, has no birthdate listed.
(See their brother Joseph Miller notes for details.)

Ellen and her sister Ruby were put in the care of E.H. Pilgrim on July 19, 1912. Their new home was four miles north of Manchester, Iowa. Mr. Pilgrim worked farming 240-acres one mile from the local school and was of the Protestant faith. The Pilgrims had two daughters aged eighteen and twenty-five and a son aged thirteen.

Violet was taken in by Arther Frank Slack on July 22, 1912. Mr. Slack resided eight-blocks northeast in the town of Manchester, Iowa. The family was of the Methodist Episcopal faith living five-blocks from the local school. Their income was from working as an iceman living in an eight-room house.

Dorothy Morris, case number 9041, was born in Luzerne, N.Y. on April 26,1912. Her father, Louis Vauranklin, worked as a laborer. Her mother was Ella Morris of Glen Falls, N.Y. Dorothy was surrendered by her mother to the superintendent of the poor in Warren County, N.Y. The date was not recorded when she joined the Henry Ocker family in the town of Manchester, Iowa. Mr. Ocker was a retired farmer living in an eight-room home.

Manson, Iowa

Marie Marguard, case number 9504, was born in Brooklyn, N.Y. on February 4, 1903. Her parents were Charles and Annie Marguard. Charles was of German descent and had died. Annie died on November 10, 1910. Marie had a sister, Helen who resided at 47 Fourth Avenue, Brooklyn, N.Y. and an uncle, a farmer, Frederick Marguard, who lived at 879 Nancock Street, Brooklyn, N.Y., and worked on a farm at Holbrook, Long Island. Marie was taken to live two and a half miles southeast of Munson, Iowa with the family of W.T. McLaughlin on January 21, 1916. The McLaughlin's had four children living one and a half miles from the local school. Mr. McLaughlin works his own 240-acre farm living in a seven-room house.

Mapleton, Iowa

Floyd Allen, case number 3710, was born in 1900. There is no other information regarding his background. In 1907 he was put in the care of F.T. George who resided one block in the town of Mapleton, Iowa. Mr. George worked as a carpenter residing near the local school in an eight-room home. There is a notation that case worker Mrs. Padellford visited him in 1917.

Emma Graham, case number 10379, was born on September 3, 1906, to David Graham who worked as a driver and was of Irish descent. His whereabouts were unknown. Emma's mother was Rachel Colwell who had died in a hospital. Emma had a sister, Sidney, who resided on Randall's Island, N.Y.C. The

CAS worker picked her up from Hope Farm. The date of her placement in the home of F.T. George was not recorded. She is placed in the same home as Floyd Allen and Mrs. Padellford, a CAS worker, visited her also in 1917.

Mason City, Iowa
Helen Frances, case number 8317, was born in N.Y.C. on May 8, 1900. There is no mention of her parents. Her city number is listed as C.C., and she was in the N.Y. House for Friendless. Helen went into the care of multiple families in Iowa.

July 17, 1912, she went to live first with R.B. Palmer who resided four miles south of Osterdock, Iowa. The Palmers had three grown children, lived one mile from the school on his own 160-acre farm.

On February 24, 1914, Mrs. P.F. Fisler took her in. The Fisler's lived four miles east of Nevada, Iowa. They were farmers living in a six-room home on a rented 200-acres, two miles from the local school. The family has two boys.

July 18, 1916, she is put in the care of W.F. Smith who lives two miles northwest of Marshalltown, Iowa. The Smith's reside on their own 400-acres in eight-room house two miles from the school. They have three grown girls.

August 17, 1916, Helen is taken in by James Moore. The Moore family in their own eight-room house farming 408-acres. The family has had two grown girls and resided three quarter miles from the local school.

March 12, 1917, she then goes to live with Hugh Gilmore who resides at 511 East State Street, Mason City, Iowa. Mr. Gilmore works as a banker and owns a ten-room home near the school. He has two boys.

In May of 1917 she is then put in the care of George E. Winters living at 419 First Street Southeast, Mason City Iowa. The Winters owns an eight-room house and Mr. Winters also works as a banker. He has a daughter aged twenty-five and also lives near the local school.

Mimmie Smith, case number 8828, was born in Marbletown, N.Y. on August 26, 1910. Her parents were Selah M. and Elmna (Oslerhondt) Smith. Mr. Smith died, and Mimmie was placed in the Kingston Industrial Home and on July 21, 1913, was put in the care of Clarnece L. Williams who is a druggist living in Mason City, Iowa.

Frank Hermance, case number 3419, was born May 29, 1897. No other information is available on him other than he was placed in the care of John Brodie in 1905, residing in Maxwell, Iowa on the "edge of town".

Zada Redding, case number 9541, was born in Connecticut on March 11, 1903. She was the daughter of Edwin and Zada A. Redding. Her mother was born in Rhode Island. The CAS received her from the Five Points House of Industry. The mother's last known address was 67 East 101st Street, N.Y.C. In February 1917 she was placed in the care of George M. Moore. The Moore family lived three miles north of Maxwell, Iowa at RFD #3. They rented a seven-room house and have three children. A visit by the CAS worker on July 25, 1917, indicates she is in the seventh grade but has unpleasant habits. She returned to N.Y.C. on August 23, 1917.

Minnesota

Elmer Martin, case number 8890, was born in Brooklyn on July 2, 1909, to Elmer G. and Sadie Martin. Mr. Martin worked as a bricklayer and turned the son over to the CAS on August 14, 1913, after the mother had died. Young Elmer was taken in by Chaus L. Hanson living in Brooten, Minnesota.

James L. Mack, case number 9503, was born in Newark, N.J. on August 30, 1905. His parents were Henry and Minette Mack. Henry had died and was of Irish descent, worked as a letter carrier. His mother's whereabouts is unknown, and she was of English descent. Both mother and father are listed as being improper guardians, intemperate. James was at the Five Points House of Industry when he was taken on October 26, 1914, to live with Charles J. Berg a few blocks from the depot in Dunnell, Minnesota. Mr. Berg owned a-lot with a five-room house near the school and attended the Lutheran church.

Walter Davison, case number 9499, has no information on his birth or parents. He was turned over to the Five Points House of Industry by Magistrate Wyatt on January 13, 1911. Rudalph Stade took him into his home on October 26, 1914, who resided eight miles north of Estherville, Iowa in the town of Dunnell, Minnesota. Mr. Stade owns 200-acres of land and lived in a nine-room house. The local school is just a half mile from their home, they are of the Lutheran faith and have five girls.

Selena Travers, case number 8969, was born in N.Y.C. on March 30, 1904, to Benjamin and Catherine Travers. After Catherine's death Selena was taken to Five Points House of Industry on October 20, 1913. Walter E. Hills took Selena in on August 7, 1916. The Hills lived two miles northeast of Eagle Lake, Minnesota. The family lived in an eight-room house. They owned 80-acres of that Mr. Hills farmed. The house set 40-rods from the local school, they attended the Seventh-Day Adventist and had a boy aged fifteen and a girl aged eighteen.

Archie Shepherd, case number 8637, was born in Bangon, N.Y. on April 28, 1901. His father was "probably a farmer." The parents were Arthur and Sarah (Warden) Shephard. Sarah was sent to the Onondaga Prison for intoxication when Archie was sent to the United Helpers Home in Ogdensburg, N.Y. As a child he had Chicken Pox. In 1913 he was placed with Mr. Nels Gunval in Ridgeway, Iowa. Before 1917 he went to live with H.E. Jones in Ellendale, Minnesota, where he was working for wages.

Victor Hempstead, case number 9501, was born on March 16, 1908, in Cairo, N.Y. His parents were Harvey and Gertrude Hempstead. Victor was committed to the Troy Orphan Asylum by Justice of the Peace, E.C. Hollenback of Green County, N.Y. On October 23, 1914, he was taken in by J.W. Tisher who lived in the town of Wallingford, Iowa. On April 10, 1915, he was then in the care of R.J. Wilcox who resided seven miles southwest of Fairmont, Minnesota, at RFD #7. Mr. Wilcox farmed 314-acres that he rented. They lived in a six-room house and had a nine-year-old child.

William H. Conley, case number 8817, was born on November 22, 1908, at his parents' residence of 133 East 45th Street, N.Y.C. He was born to Harry John and Elizabeth (Walker) Conley. Mr.

Conley worked as a hotel clerk and when his wife died the CAS took William. On July 17, 1917, Oscar F. Ulland took him in. The Ulland's lived in town in Fergus Falls, Minnesota. Mr. Ulland worked as a banker and lived in a ten-room town home just blocks from the church. They attended the Presbyterian church.

Sophia Anderson, case number 9497, was born November 10, 1904. Her parents were Frank and Lizzie Anderson. Frank was from Norway and Lizzie from Ireland. Frank deserted the family, and Sophia was sent to the Church Charity Foundation. On November 8, 1915, she was taken in by Henry C. Bauer residing two miles south of Nerstrand, Minnesota at RFD #2 Kenyon Minnesota. They were farming 120 rented-acres living in a six-room home. Their house was a half mile from the school, and they attended the Lutheran church.

Lillian Heaney, case number 8888, was born in Kingston, N.Y. on January 24, 1903. She had measles and scarlet fever; no information is available on who her parents were. She was put in the Kingston Industrial School, N.Y. on September 16, 1913. She was taken in by Hano A. Bendickson who resided four miles east of Emmons, Minnesota, on April 27, 1913. The local school was 80-rods from their home. Mr. Bendickson farmed 119-acres and had two children. No date was given; she was then moved in with Rufus Bisbee family two and a half miles south of London, Minnesota, they lived in the town of Lyle Minnesota. Mr. Bisbee had six children and lived in a seven-room house on 107-acres.

Leon Floyd Hodge, case number 8557, was born in Corning, N.Y. on April 14, 1907. His parents were Floyd and Louise (Dixon) Hodge. He had a sister Frances Hodge. Leon was surrendered by his mother to the Poor Master, Corning, N.Y. on August 3, 1912. He was taken in by Robert W. Smith who lived thirteen miles north of Decorah, Iowa in Mabel, Minnesota. The Smiths lived three quarters of a mile from the local school and owned an 80-acre farm.

Eleanor Ricketts, case number 8825, was born in Glen Falls, N.Y. on October 21, 1908, to Charles J. and Louise (Decker) Ricketts. The CAS workers picked her up from the

Superintendent of Poor in Warrensburg, N.Y. On July 21, 1913, she was placed with the family of Henry C. Wolf in the suburbs of Myrtle, Minnesota.

Catherine Graves, case number 10087, was born in Waverly, N.Y. to George and June C. (Gavin) Graves on March 14, 1908. Mr. Graves worked as a laborer and lived in Barton, N.Y. Catherine was taken to the Southern Tier Orphanage in Elmira, N.Y. on September 1, 1914. On December 21, 1915, she was put in the care of Mrs. Julia Brick who lived six miles east of Ellendale, Minnesota at RFD #1 New Richmond, Minnesota. The Brick's owned a 160-acre farm living in an eight-room house a quarter mile from the school. They attended the Catholic church and had one boy aged fifteen.

Robert Schultz, case number 8321, was born on December 2, 1906, in N.Y.C., to John and Lillian Schultz. He was abandoned at the home of Mrs. O. Connell on 319 East 75th Street in the City and taken to the N.Y. Nursery and Children's Hospital. Childhood diseases are listed as Measles and Chicken Pox. Robert was taken in by Matthew Johnson who resides four miles west and four miles north of Ostrander, Minnesota at an RFD. The distance/direction is also listed as six miles north and two miles east of Chester, Minnesota. The Johnson's owned an 80-acre farm attended the Methodist Episcopal church. Their eight-room house was one and a half miles from the school.

Cora DeRocher, case number 3412, was born in Rochester, N.Y. on October 12, 1900. Her mother is listed as Mrs. F. Kramer who resided in Farmington, N.Y. No date is recorded on when she joined Jacob Divas' household. The Divas lived seven miles from Spring Valley, Minnesota at RFD #6. Their house consisted of eight-rooms near the school. The Family attended the Methodist Episcopal church and owned 8-acres.

John Stanber, case number 7225, was born on January 4, 1900. The notes read that his father is dead, and the mother's name is Marie. He was taken by the CAS on October 24, 1910, picked up at 413 West 23rd Street, N.Y.C. Mr. Bert A. Tellefsen took him in, residing nine miles northeast of Walnut Grove, Minnesota at RFD #1. Mr. Tellefsen was a farmer who attended the Lutheran church. They owned 400-acres of land, living in a seven-room house one mile from the local school.

Henry Schroeder, case number 8564, was born in Brooklyn, N.Y. to German immigrants Henry and Lizzie (Makie) Schroeder on December 31, 1901. Lizzie died and Henry was placed in the Brooklyn Orphan Asylum Society on January 28, 1913. On September 9, 1916, he was placed in the care of Gustave Dunse residing seven miles south of Windom, Minnesota at RFD #4. Mr. Dunse occupation was farming and lived in a six-room home a mile from the school. He was of the Lutheran faith and had four girls.

Edna Hudson, case number 4541, was born March 3rd, 1905, in the N.Y. Infant Asylum. Her parents were Benjamin and Emma Hudson. Her mother surrendered her to the N.Y. Infant Asylum on January 7, 1907. (It's noted that she died.) On January 15, 1907, Edna was placed in the care of Ernest Snare of RFD #2 Winnebago, Minnesota living eight and a half miles northeast of town.

Frederick Winkleman, case number 8896, was born on March 9, 1899, in Brooklyn. His city number was A-392 and parents were Charles and Wilhemina (Urader) Winkleman. Wilhemina died and Frederick was placed in the Sterling Place Home on August 15, 1913. As a child he had scarlet fever. On September 26, 1913, he was placed in the care of Henry Wolf of Myrtle, Minnesota. The family was of the Lutheran faith renting a nine-room house on 160-acres.

Monona, Iowa

Louise Miller, case number 8151, was born in N.Y.C. on July 15, 1907. Her parents were Walter and Annie Miller. Childhood disease is listed as whooping cough. There was no date recorded when she was taken in by Martin Frank who lived five miles north of Monona, Iowa. Mr. Frank owned 140-acres of land.

Nevada, Iowa

Committee

Mrs. L.H. Padellford

Anna Crapo, case number 10722, was born on April 19, 1905. She was born to Isaac and Eva (Lewis) Crapo. Isaac worked as a laborer and had died. Eva remarried Charles Parks of Corning, N.Y. Due to bad home conditions Anna was taken to the Southern Tier Orphan Asylum in Elmira, N.Y. On October 12, 1917, she was put in the care of H.R. Irish who lived in the town of Forest City, Iowa. Mr. Irish was a physician and owned a ten-room house near the school. The attended the Methodist Episcopal church and had a 20-year-old son. On January 19, 1918, she was then taken to live with Charles Johnson four miles southwest of Ames, Iowa at RFD #3. Mr. Ames was a farmer owning 105-acres living in an eight-room house near the school. They also attended the Methodist Episcopal church and had an 18-year-old son. Then on July 5, 1918, she was taken in by Earl Kirkindall who resides five and a half miles southeast of Navada, Iowa. Mr. Kirkindall also works farming and owned 18-acres and a seven-room house. The family consisted of a boy and two girls. Like the Kirkindall's they lived near their local school and attended the Methodist Episcopal church.

Douglas J. Price, case number 10511, was born on November 20, 1909, in Gloversville, N.Y. His parents were George and Annie Price. His father was employed as a mason tender. The family resided at 38 Thompson Avenue, Gloversville, N.Y. Douglas was surrendered by his parents as they were deemed "improper guardians." On March 7, 1917, Paul Ruchlow took him in. Mr. Ruchlow lived five miles west of St. Ansgar, Iowa at RFD #1. They were of the Lutheran faith living three quarter miles from the school. The home consisted of seven-rooms on a 160 rented farm. There is a note that in September of 1917, he was living with Mrs. W. Star. No other information regarding the Star family is available. On October 12, 1917, he then went to live with Henry Schultz living one mile west and a half mile north of Leland, Iowa at RFD #2 Forest City, Iowa. Mr. Schultz worked at farming and rented 160-acres. He too had a seven-room house one mile from the school and was of the Methodist Episcopal faith with a daughter aged five. Douglas later went to live with O.W. Johnson ten miles west of Lansing, Iowa. The

Johnson's owed a 160-acre farm and an eight-room house. From there Douglas went to H.B. Mallory farm two and a half miles west of Ames, Iowa. The Mallory's also owned a 160-acre farm and lived in an eight-room house.

Clarence Sonson, case number 8172, was born on September 10, 1913, in Brooklyn.
Mabel Sonson, case number 8173, was born in Brooklyn on June 19, 1900.
They were the children of Sweden immigrants of the Protestant faith. His parents were Gustave and Selma Sonson, and both died. He was placed in the Orphan Asylum Society. The father died of tuberculosis and had a brother "out west."

Clarence first went to live with Isane Cougher on May 1, 1912. They owed 200-acres and had a ten-room house, attended the Methodist Episcopal church. The Cougher's lived three miles south of Colo, Iowa. Then on May 19, 1912, he was taken in by William Paul, who farmed, and resided three and a quarter mile northeast of Nevada, Iowa at RFD #3. Then in September 1917, Asa McConnell, a Janitor became his guardian. Mr. McConnell lived in the town of Nevada, Iowa.

Mabel went to live with the family of William Hague on May 1, 1912. The first lived two miles south of Nevada. The Hagues owned 160-acres that they farmed. The lived in a ten-room house and attended the Methodist Episcopal church. In the fall of 1914, they moved into town.

Glen B. Watson, case number 10517, no birthdate is given. (See his brother, Evert.) He also had a brother Glen. On March 6, 1917, he was put in the care of Jerry E. Irvin living three miles west and five miles south of Marble Rock, Iowa in Green, Iowa. Mr. Irvin rented a six-room house a quarter mile from the local school and worked farming. On May 17, 1917, he was then placed with James Brooks four miles north and two miles east of Colo, Iowa at RFD #3 Nevada, Iowa. The Brooks owned 300-acres living in an eight-room house one mile from the local school. They attended the Methodist Episcopal church and had two daughters ages 14 and 19.

Viola Schoonmaker, case number 8433, was born in Esopus, N.Y. on April 18, 1902. (See sister Maude.) In May 1917, she was put in the care of James Moore, living five miles northeast of Armstrong, Iowa. The Moore's lived in a rented nine-room home on 400-acres working as a farmer, one mile from the school. On October 23, 1917, she then went to live with Roy Carlson who lived in the same neighborhood. Mr. Carlson also farmed and rented 160-acres with a nine-room home three miles from the church and school. Viola was then taken in by Mrs. L.H. Paddellfood on August 3, 1918. The family resided in the town of Nevada, Iowa. They owned an eight-room house three blocks from the school and three blocks from the church.

New Albion, Iowa

Louise Siani, case number 8373, was of Italian descent born in N.Y.C. on May 7, 1903. Her parents were Sabato and Louisa (Brusciono) Siani. On March 15, 1912, she was placed with Miss Carter of N.Y.C. Mission. Then on December 12, 1912, she was placed in the care of James Burke who lives in a seven-room home in New Albin, Iowa. The James family attended the Catholic church.

New Sharon, Iowa there are no pages behind this tab.
North Dakota
Jamestown, N.D.

Dorothy Alexander, case number 9235, was born about 1910 in Gouverneur, N.Y. to Robert and Violet (West) Alexander. Her parents were both born in Vermont, and she has a brother, Guy. The children were placed in the United Helpers Home on March 20, 1914. Dorothy was taken in by Charles W. and Irene Bitner of Jamestown, N.D. Mr. Bitner owed a house near the school, attended the Presbyterian church, worked as a Salesman, and had a daughter aged ten.

Leo Dyer, case number 9238, was born on September 14, 1901, to Albert and Mary Dyer. He had a brother, Albert. On April 27, 1917, he went to live with Andrew Johnson Bayles six miles north of Jamestown, N.D. Mr. Bayles worked as a farmer renting 320-acres. They lived in a five-room home two and a half miles from the school. On June 13, 1915, he then went to live with the Isenburg family five miles north of Jamestown, N.D. The Isenburg family attended the local Union church and also lived two and a half miles from their school and owned 200-acres that they farmed.

LeRoy Huestis, case number 9238, was born in N.Y.C. on January 8, 1908. He was the son of Frederick and Jennie Huestis. LeRoy had in his early years measles and was placed in the Home for Friendless on December 13, 1911. On April 27, 1914, he went to the home of Andrew and Florence May Roedel at 210 Sixth Street, Jamestown, N.D. Andrew Roedel was a Missionary with the seventh-day Adventists and owned a four-room house near the school. On November 4, 1914, he then went into the care of Thomas Soren who worked farming on their 160-acres. They lived two miles from the school and was of the Protestant faith living nine miles north and one mile west at RFD #1, Buchanan, N.D. On May 19, 1916, they moved twelve miles north of Jamestown, N.D. to RFD #2 Cleveland, N.D. Here Mr. Soren purchased 160-acres and continues farming, living three miles from the school.

John Otto, case number 9242, was born in N.Y.C. on November 20, 1907. His parents were from N.Y.C and are John and Victoria Otto. On January 26, 1914, he was put in the N.Y. Infant Asylum Home for Friendless. On April 27, 1914, he then went to live with Louis C. and Emily L. Moore. Mr. Moore was a veterinary owning his home in the town of Jamestown, N.D. near the school and attended the Methodist church. The Moore's had three boys, aged six, fifteen, & eighteen and two girls, aged twelve and twenty.

Mary Smith, case number 9243, was born in Reynoldsville, N.Y. on October 18, 1901.
Rose Smith, case number 9244, was born in Corning, N.Y. on April 18, 1908.
Their father was from Bennettsburg, N.Y. and Mother from Cayutaville, N.Y. They were Charles and Florence (Havens) Smith. Mr. Smith worked as a Laborer, and they were of the Presbyterian faith. Mary had a sister, Rose, and the girls were placed in care of the Superintendent of Poor of Schuyler County, on December 22, 1913. On April 27th both girls were put in the care of John J. and Mary E. Lotta who lived in the town of Jamestown, N.D. Mr. Lotta was a Presbyterian Minister and

owned his home near the school. On May 20, 1916, the girls split up.

Mary went to live with O.C. & Annie M. Johnson (ages forty-nine & 42) at 118 East Wisconsin Street, Jamestown, N.D. Mr. Johnson was an insurance agent, owned his house living four blocks from the school. On April 12, 1917, she then was taken in by Reverend Willaim Graham residing at RFD #2 Ryder, N.D. Directions are one and a half mile north, eleven miles east, and one and a quarter mile west. Mr. Graham is a retired Presbyterian Minister living in a five-room house and owns 200-acres. Then on August 12, 1918, she goes to live with Mrs. Matthew Johnson eight and a half miles northeast of Chester, N.D.

Rose went to live with J. Reynolds and Ionia Anderson. Mr. Reynolds is a firefighter who owns a home in at 316 Third Avenue North, Jamestown, N.D. His house is two blocks from the school and attend the Presbyterian church. They have a six your old boy.

Margaret Miller, case number 9798, was born in Naruassing, N.Y. on June 15, 1912.
Mary Miller, case number 9240, was born on June 30, 1911, also in Naruassing, N.Y.
Rose Miller, case number 9241, was born on February 1, 1909. All three girls were illegitimate children of John Miller and Carrie Kromgrate. The remarks in the records read: Father, drunken, dishonest, unfortunate. Mother, feeble minded in Custodial Asylum, Newark. Family, low and degraded. All three girls were taken in by Oscar S. Zimmerman on April 19, 1915. Mr. Zimmerman is a merchant that owns his business and home and lives near the school. The family is of the Methodist faith, has a housekeeper living with them and has three girls, ages 5, 7, & 9.

Ernest Wells, case number 9245, was born on September 10, 1903
Louis Wells, case number 9246, was born on November 14, 1906
The two boys were born to Jessie Wells, no father is mentioned. There are no notes on what happened, but the CAS picked them

up from the Troy Orphan Asylum. On April 27, 1914, both boys went to live with Herman F. and Frieda Stine living seven miles north of Jamestown, N.D. The Stines owned 640-acres, farming two miles from the local school and were of the Lutheran faith. They had a 10-month-old daughter. On June 24, 1917, they began living with Olson Wells, whose address is also Jamestown, N.D. There are no notations if Olson is related or just coincidence that the last name is the same. Louis then on July 3, 1917, went into the care of Leone Brown, and on May 4, 1918, with Edwin Frey. The notes do not indicate that Ernest moved after being placed with Olson Wells.

Northwood, Iowa
July 22, 1913, Committee
Dr. Hurd
Dr. Dwelle
Eckert
Toye, a banker
Hangen
Kepler
Thompson

Clifford Eugene Adair, case number 8814, was born in Hobart, N.Y. on July 12, 1907. His parents were Claude and Edna (Brownell) Adair. Mr. Adair worked as a laborer and they lived in Arbeville, N.Y. Clifford was taken to Orra Cain, overseer of the poor in Gilboa, N.Y. On July 15, 1913, he was taken to live with John Freitag who lives four and a half miles west and one and a half miles south of Kensett, Iowa. Mr. Freitag owns a 124-acre farm and lives in an eight-room house a half mile from the church and is of the Lutheran faith.

George Black, case number 8815, was born in N.Y.C. on April 19, 1910.
Rose Black, case number 8816, was born on October 5, 1907, in N.Y.C.
Lawrence Black, case number 8887, was b on November 28, 1912, in N.Y.C.
Their parents were to Charles and Katherine (Thorp) Black. Mr. Black worked as a chauffeur. The children were turned over to the CAS by their father. Both Parents were still alive when the CAS took them.

George was taken to Northwood, Iowa in the care of Edward K. Pitman on July 22, 1913. Mr. Pitman was the editor of the newspaper and owned a-lot with an eight-room house just two blocks from the school. He was of the Methodist Episcopal faith.

Rose was taken on July 24, 1917, to live with Willie Struck one and a half miles north of Northwood, Iowa. Mr. Struck rented a farm and a six-room home one and a half miles from the school and was of the Lutheran faith.

Lawrence was placed with his sister, Rose, in the care of the Willie Struck family.

Ruth Glover, case number 8893, was born on April 22, 1906. The names of the parents are not noted but there is a notation that the mother was dead, dying of consumption. Ruth has a sister that lives in Dundee and a blind sister in Batavia State School. The Elks care for the blind girl. On September 22, 1913, Thomas Evans takes Ruth into this home where his family lives a half mile south of Joice, Iowa. Mr. Evans works on an 80-acre farm living in a seven-room house. They are of the Lutheran faith, live a half mile from the local school and have two children.

Viola Palmer, case number 10510, was born in Kingston, N.Y. on February 13, 1910. (See sister's Gladys, Stella, and Ruth Palmer notes.) On March 1, 1917, Viola was placed with Frank Mahoney who's a Real Estate Salesman living one mile south of Charles City, Iowa. Mr. Mahoney owns 10-acres with an eight-room house one mile from the school. He has a 4-year-old boy. On May 17, 1917, she is taken in by E.G. Harmon who resides ten miles south of Northwood, Iowa. Mr. Harmon owns his farm consisting of 160-acrs. He is of the Lutheran faith, has a an 8-year-old son and the school is on his property.

Harry Partington, case number 8823, was born in Peekskill, N.Y. on June 23, 1903. His parents were James William and Ella (Smith) Partington. James worked as a firefighter for Marlborough, N.Y. and Ella died. There are no dates noted but Harry was put in the care of E.G. Johnson who lived three miles west and four miles south of Kessett, Iowa. The family was Lutherans, had two boys and lived one mile from the school. Mr. Johnson worked as a farmer, and they lived in a seven-room house.

John Edward Ricketts, case number 8826, was born in Glen Falls, N.Y. on February 2, 1911. His parents were Charles J. and Louise (Decker) Ricketts. Charles worked as a meat cutter. The Superintendent of Poor from Warrensburg, N.Y. turned him over to the CAS. On July 23, 1913, he went to live with Oscar Low. Oscar lived in town and owned a seven-room house, worked as a grocer, and attended the Lutheran church.

Walter Smith, case number 8829, was born in Marbletown, N.Y. on May 24, 1908. (See his sister's notes, Mimmie Smith.) On July 22, 1913, he went to live with Eddie G. Harmon in Northwood, Iowa. The Harmons lived in an eight-room house and owned a 160-acre farm. They were of the Lutheran faith and lived 10-rods from the school.

Willie Tinger, case number 8895, was born in Brooklyn, N.Y. on September 8, 1902. His father was Harry Duncan of Long Island City and Mother Nellie Tinger Riha. Paternity not legally established before mother's death. Grandfather is able but refuses to care for child. Willie was turned over to the Commissioner of Charities in Schenectady, N.Y. Willie was taken in by Lois A. Aurdahl who resides at RFD #1 living nine miles northeast of Carpenter, Iowa. The family had one girl and owned 120-acres where they were engaged in farming. Living in a seven-room house, they were Lutherans, and the school was on their farm.

Milton Winkleman, case number 8897, was born in Brooklyn on January 28, 1904, to Charles and Wilhelmina (Urader) Winkleman. His mother died and he was city number A-393 taken to the Brooklyn Infant S. Asylum and Home for D.C. On September 25, 1913, he was put in the care of Rudalph Virchow who lived seven miles north of Northwood, Iowa. The Virchow's lived in an eight-room house one mile from the school. Mr. Virchow worked as a farmer and was of the Lutheran faith.

Henry Forbes, case number 10143, was born on November 28, 1914. His N.Y.C. number is A-8537, from Bellevue Hospital. The remarks indicate that Henry is "A Foundling." (An infant that has been abandoned by its parents and is discovered and cared for by others.) As a child Henry had measles, and the CAS picked him up from the Nursery and Childs Hospital. He was put in the care of Guy T. Alchorn who lives one and a half miles southwest of Osage, Iowa. Mr. Alchorn owns a six-room house, works as a mail carrier, attends the Methodist Episcopal Church, and has a 17-year-old daughter.

Mary Graham, case number 10380, was born on June 21, 1909, to David and Rachael (Colwell) Graham. David worked as a driver, and Rachel is listed as dead. Mary has a sister, Sidney, who lives on Roadells Island, N.Y. Mary was at Hope Farm when taken west and put with the Frank Annis family on November 2, 1917. Mr. Annis lived in town five blocks from the depot and owned an eleven-room house. He worked as the manager of a lumber company; they resided near the school and attended the Congregational Church.

Bertha Kacin, case number 10382, was born on June 11, 1902.
Louise Kacin, case number 10381, was born on February 7, 1911.
The girls had a brother, Joseph and sister, Anna lived in the town of Zearing, Iowa.
Their parents were Joseph and Anna Kacin, who lived at 508 East 70th Street in N.Y.C. Anna died in 1913. The children were turned over to the CAS workers from their father. On October 18, 1916,

Bertha was taken in by Clark Gardner who lived in the town of Osage, Iowa, they ran a nursery and attended the Baptist church. He has a ten-room house.

Louise was taken in by Charles F. Gardner who lived in the town of Osage, Iowa, they ran a nursery and attended the Baptist church. He also has a ten-room house.

Henry Wilson, case number 10385, was born to John and Frances Wilson on September 26, 1909. John worked as a sailor and had died, Frances lived at 145 East 126th Street, N.Y.C. Henry was sent to the Five Points House of Industry before going to live with W.C. Gardner on October 17, 1916. The W.C. Gardner family lives in the town of Osage, Iowa, they own a ten-room house near the school. Mr. Gardner works as a Nursery Man and has two girls. (It's assumed that the three Gardner men, Clark, Charles F. and W.C., are brothers and work together in the Nursery.)

Harry Maxwell, case number 10383, was born on August 24, 1900.
Robert Maxwell, case number 10384, was born in August of 1912. (no day of month listed)
The boys were taken to the Hope Farm where the CAS picked them up. Their grandfather was Thomas Maxwell who resided at 547 South 4th Street, N.Y.C. They also had a cousin, Mrs. E. Holbran residing at 630 Tenth Avenue, N.Y.C.

Harry was put in the care of Fred Stallman who lived nine miles northeast of Osage, Iowa and two- and three-quarter miles north of Little Cadar, Iowa in Osage, Iowa. Mr. Stallman owned 120-acres, worked farming, and lived in a six-room house. They attended the Congregational Church and lived two- and three-quarter miles from school.

Robert went on October 19, 1916, to live with John P. Wright fifteen miles southeast of Orchard, Iowa at RFD #1. The Wright family lived in a ten-room house and farmed 240-acres which they owned. Their house was one- and three-quarter miles from the school and they were of the Methodist Episcopal faith.

Osceola, Iowa

Tracy Emick, case number 3023, was born on May 16, 1902, in Elmira Hights, N.Y. to Thomas and Julia (Stage) Emick. When Mr. & Mrs. Emick separated, Tracy was sent to the Southern Tier Orphan Home in Elmira, N.Y. On October 18, 1904, Tracy was taken in by Clarence Carder who lives four miles north and five miles west of Osceola, Iowa at RFD #2. The family lives in a six-room house six-rods from the school, farming 160-acres. They attend the Methodist Episcopal church.

William Decker, case number 3084, was born May 16, 1901. There is no mention of who his mother was, he was placed in the Kingston Industrial School just after his father, George, died. In 1916 he was put in the care of Floyd Frombley who resides in Osceola, Iowa.

Andrew Gulicksen, case number 8101, was born April 5, 1902, the son of Andrew and Aagodt (Gunderson) Gulicksen. Andrew had a brother, Louis and sister, Anna. He was placed in the Home for Destitute Children. On July 15, 1912, J.W. Elder took him in. Mr. Elder lives in Manchester, Iowa. He farms 300-acres which he rents. They live in a seven-room house a quarter mile from the school and attend the Baptist church.

Ida Johnson, case number 2704, was born in N.Y. on November 15, 1899. His parents were of the protestant faith, and both born in Sweden. She became a ward of the city June 12, 1902, and placed in the "Children's Fold" – and it's noted she had no visitors. Ida was in the care of James McComas how lived in the town of Osceola, Iowa. A notation on June 10, 1916, indicates she completed a 12th grade education.

Helen Kitchen, case number 6365, was born in N.Y.C. on August 31, 1899.
Henrietta Kitchen, case number 6366, was born in N.Y.C. on January 14, 1904. Their parents were George and Henrietta (Feraday) Kitchen. The parents are of the Presbyterian faith, George was from Maine and worked as a truck driver. The mom was from Pennsylvania. The girls were surrendered by mom who lived at 432 East 139th Street in the City. Their father deserted the family, has had a term on the island for non-support.

Helen was first place in the home of R.J. Jewell on September 21, 1909, three blocks north and one-block west of Plainview, Nebraska. The Jewell family lived two blocks from the school in a large house. Mr. Jewell owned a Marble business and has grown children. On October 6, 1910, she then went into the family of J.W. Fickel, three quarters of miles north of Osceola, Iowa. Mr. Fickel owned a farm, and their house had six-rooms, three quarters of a miles from the school. They attended the Methodist church and had two sons.

Henrietta was first placed on September 21, 1909, with Charles Ulerich who lives three blocks north and one-block west of Plainview, Nebraska. Mr. Ulerich worked as a Butcher. Then on August 18, 1910, she joined J.B. Newman's family residing three miles north of Osceola, Iowa at RFD #1. February 15, 1912, E.A. Gordon took her in. He resided one and a half miles north of Osceola, Iowa. Mr. Gordon farmed owning 120-acres. The Gordon's resided one and a half miles from the school and church and had one child. Henrietta was adopted by the Gordon family on May 21, 1916.

August Brennison, case number 2188, was born in Brooklyn on October 28, 1897. His parents were August G. and Mary Brennison. The father deserted the family. In December 1902, he was taken in by H. Schwartz who lived in the town of Plainview, Minnesota.

Rock Rapids, Iowa
Committee
Dr. George H. Boetel
C.C. Brugman, Druggist
Simon Fisher, District Attorney
W.S. Wilson, Superintendent of Schools
W.G Smith, Editor
E.L. Partch, Banker
W.S. Cooper, Grocer
H.B. Pierce, Real Estate

Mable Krauss, case number 8559, was born in N.Y.C. on December 16, 1902. (See her brother, Harold Krauss.) They also had a sister Mildred. Mable's city number was A-368. All three children were originally placed in the same household. On April 3, 1913, Mable was moved to the home of Mrs. Elizabeth Albers. Mrs. Albers lived one mile southwest of Cresco, Iowa and owned a cottage type home one mile from the school. She has two grown boys.   No date given when Mable then moved to the home of Carl Brugman who lived in the town of Rock Rapids, Iowa. The visits from the CAS are dated June 29, 1916, and February 12, 1917, which indicates she is in the seventh grade. The last notation on Mable (with no date) is she returned to N.Y.C. for medical treatment.

Gladys Wilson, case number 10730, was born on September 22, 1909. Her father was T. Archers and mother Hattie Peeters. When mom died, she was sent to the Ontario Orphan Asylum. Gladys had chicken pox, and her Tonsils and Adenoids removed when she was young. Mrs. William Larwood of New Haven, N.Y. is an aunt and Miss Kolor, Superintendent of the Institution said aunt was a good woman. Gladys was first placed on October 12, 1917, with Rev. Alvis L. McMillan who resided in the town of Forest City, Iowa six blocks east of the railroad station. Rev. McMillan preached at the Baptist church and was the father of a nine-year-old girl.   The family lived in the eight-room parsonage near the local school. On April 22, 1918, she went to live with Henry Stonecipher in the town of Earlville, Iowa. Mr. Stonecipher was a minister of the Methodist Episcopal faith and owned a seven-room house. There is no date mentioned when she went then went to live with the family of Fred Tilstra of Rock Rapids, Iowa. They lived in town three-blocks east and two blocks north of the station.

Edward Blair, case number 10904, was born on April 9, 1910, in Auburn, N.Y. His parents are unknown, and the CAS received him from Maud B. Booth, of the Salvation Army at 34 West 28th Street, N.Y.C. On November 21, 1918. He was put in the care of Fred Schemmel residing one mile from Rock Rapids, Iowa and the mailing address was Box 147. Mr. Schemmel farmed 470-acres and lived in a nine-room house.

Wilson Barnhart, case number 10905, was born January 31, 1918, to Cora Barnhart. His father is unknown. The CAS got him from the Superintendent of Poor, J. Smith Brundage. Burton J. Sherman became his caregiver on June 29, 1918.   The

Sherman's resided in the town of Rock Rapids, Iowa. Mr. Sherman works as a contractor and rents his home.

Rachael B. Jones, case number 10907, was born in Saxton, N.Y. on December 25, 1913.
Bertha A. Jones, case number 10906, was born in Catskill, N.Y. on November 26, 1915.
Their parents never married. The father was Stephen Jones, a laborer from Hunter, N.Y. The mother was from Maryville, N.Y. and was Hannah A. Cole. After the parents separated Hannah could no longer support the children. The notes indicate that Stephen was intemperate and shiftless. On June 28, 1918, Jans Vickers took in both girls. The Vickers lived a half mile from Little Rock, Iowa owning their seven-room house on 380-acres. The local school was a half mile away.

Roy Kilmer, case number 10908, was born May 20, 1908, in Jackson Corners, N.Y. to William and Julia (Ingles) Kilmer. William worked as a farm laborer, Julia was from Poughkeepsie, N.Y. Notes indicate that Roy's father was abusive, and his mother was immoral when he was placed in the care of the State Charities Aid Association. On June 25, 1918, Roy went to live with E. Freyberg who lived one mile east and forty roads south of Lester, Iowa. Mr. Freyberg rented a six-room house on a 320-acre farm. They resided a half mile from the school and one mile from the local church and had three other children.

Peter Lea, case number 10909, was born in Brooklyn, N.Y. on January 24, 1906. Peter's childhood diseases are listed as Measles, Pertussis, and he had his Tonsils removed. His father was a general utility man at the Erie Basin Dry Dock. Both his parents Peter and Emma (Lievre) Lea had died, and the CAS received Peter from his aunt and uncle, Mr. & Mrs. Gus Lievre who resided at 278 Palisade Avenue West Hoboken, N.Y. On June 27, 1918, Peter was taken in by Jake VanGilder who lived four miles east and two miles north of Rock Rapids, Iowa. Mr. VanGilder rented a seven-room house on 150-acres where that he farmed. VanGilder's had four girls.

Edward Risberg, case number 10910, was born in Hermsand, Sweden on May 26, 1904.

Mary Risberg, case number 10911, was born in Brooklyn, N.Y. on March 22, 1906.

The parents both Sweden immigrants died. They were Edward L. and Anna (Ketman) Risberg. Mary had chickenpox, measles, and her tonsils and adenoids removed. They had a cousin, Mrs. J.M. Higgins, who resided at RFD #1 Middletown, Connecticut. When their parents died, they were sent to the Home for Seamen's Children as there was no one to care for either of them. On June 27, 1918, Hans Raveling became their caregiver residing five and a half miles southwest of Rock Rapids, Iowa at RFD #4. Mr. Raveling worked farming, owned a six-room house on 160-acres. They resided one mile from the school and five miles from the local church.

Sidney, Iowa

George Vermilyea, case number 3264, was born June 19, 1898. His parents were Protestants from Brooklyn. They were William and Lillian (Hornbuckle) Vermilyea. Goerge was a Ward of the City and placed in the E.D.I.S. in Brooklyn. On March 16, 1905, George was put in the care of Mr. Jackson of Sidney, Iowa. There is a notation (no date) that reads: Working for wages. Bro. Chas. persuaded him to work for wages.

South Dakota

Guy Alexander, case number 9234, was born on March 19, 1913, in Gouverneur, N.Y. (See sister, Dorothy Alexander.) On April 27, 1914, he was taken in by William Benjamin Payne who resided in the town of Jamestown, North Dakota. Mr. Payne was a Minister at the Advent Church living in a six-room house near the school. The Payne's had an eight-year-old girl. On January 31, 1917, the family moved to Mountain View, Colorado. On May 14, 1917, they moved one mile southeast of Redfield, South Dakota.

Frederick Bielow, case number 6361, was born in Brooklyn on October 16, 1899.

Harry Bielow, case number 6362, was born in Brooklyn on December 12, 1901.

Frederick and Harry's parents were Charles and Lizzie (Schuler) Bielow. They were turned over to the E.D.I.S. It is noted in their records that; "Mother in home for aged and infirm, Flat Bush, Long Island. Father has broken both legs and unable to support, served time for non-support." On September 25, 1909, both boys were taken in by J.E. Shaw who lived eight miles west and one mile south of Colton, S.D. at RFD #3 Monrose, S.D. Mr. Shaw owned his own farm, and they lived in a five-room house one mile from the local school.

Mildred Cook, case number 9137, was born in Brooklyn on November 27, 1911. The whereabouts of her father are unknown. Mildred is the daughter of Robert and Annie (Brown) Cook. She was sent to the Nursery and Child's Hospital on January 28, 1914. Her grandmother was Mrs. Bertha A. Cook of 938 Newkirk Avenue, Brooklyn, N.Y. On March 15, 1914, she was taken in by Mrs. Annie E. Simmons who resided in town two blocks from the depot in Fulton, S.D. Mrs. Simmons owned a six-room house in town near the school.

Vincent J. Egan, case number 9138, was born on March 4, 1900, in N.Y.C. His parents were James and Johanna (Dillion) Egan. There is note date on this record to indicate when it was logged into Miss Comstock's book. But the notations indicates that the father was a driver of a paper wagon for S.C. Department and died. His mother is listed as being dead for 14 years. Vincent has a 16-year-old brother living with a Mrs. Condon at 870 Jennings Street, Box, N.Y. He also has a brother, (no age given) Daniel Egan, who lives at 3049 Hull Avenue, Bronx, N.Y. No date listed when the CAS took Vincent to live with G.B. Tuttle in Mt. Vernon, S.D. at RFD #4. Their house was nine miles north of Mt. Vernon or seventeen miles northwest of Mitchell, S.D.

Mary Gear, case number 9139, was born in 1901 (no day or month listed) in Schenectady, N.Y. She was institutionalized on February 3, 1911, at St. Vincents in Albany. Her family was of the Catholic faith. The notes indicate that the father is dead, and mother is "dissolute, improper guardianship." Their names are not mentioned in the records. On December 27, 1916, she is put in the care of Fred Weld who lives five and a half miles north of Salam, S.D. at RFD #1. Miss Comstock was unable to find a catholic family for Mary to join, the Weld's were Protestant living one mile from the local school. They owned a five-room house farming their 150-acres.

Walter Kirshner, case number 9140, was born on April 28, 1900, in Brooklyn to Germany immigrants Casper and Kuns (Groff) Kirshner. Walter's city number was A-351. Nothing indicates what happened to his father, his mother had been in the Kings Park Hospital for eleven years and listed as insane. Walter had a sister, Margaret, who lived at 157 First Street, Maspeth, Long Island. On April 12, 1916, Walter was taken in by Louis H. Lingschert who lives one mile north and three miles east of Parkston, South Dakota. The Lingschert's was a farming family who owned a three-room house on 160-acres one mile from the school.

Clinton Peters, and **Henry Peters:**
There are no notes that indicate where the Peters brothers came from, their parents or how they ended up with Miss Comstock headed west. There is also no case number listed. The only indication of Clinton's age is he is in the fifth grade and Henry is in the seventh grade when placed on November 2, 1917. Clinton went to live with George Luckett twenty miles west of Lacy, S.D. and thirteen south of Pierre, S.D. Mr. Luckett owned 400-acres of land.

Helen Miles, case number 9116, was born in Rathbone, N.Y. on December 24, 911.
Margaret Miles, case number 9117, was born on January 15, 1910.
Their parents were Orson and Anna B. (Covel) Miles. Orson was a farmer from Rathbone, N.Y. and Helen was from Bath, N.Y. Their mother turned them over to the CAS.
Helen was placed in the home of Sigmund Frederick and Mary Schirmer who lived four-blocks northwest of the depot in Mt. Vernon, S.D. Her new family was of the Methodist faith owning their own house near the school. Mr. Frederick worked as a banker.

Margaret was placed with Thomas Nerland on March 19, 1914, who lived eighteen miles from Ru Heights, S.D.

Howard Pearke, case number 9141, was born on September 12, 1904. His parents are both listed as deceased, and he was turned over to a CAS worker by the Rev. Eli Pitman. On March 18, 1914, he was put in the care of B. Frank Licherknecht who lived four miles southeast of Esther, S.D. and sixteen miles Southeast of Mitchell, S.D. at RFD #1 Ethan, S.D. Mr. Licherknecht worked farming on 160-acre rented property. They lived in a five-room house a quarter mile from the school and was of the Methodist Episcopal faith.

Edward Smith, case number 1942, was born in Armonk, N.Y. on December 19, 1908. His parents were Samuel and Etta (Dayton) Smith. His father worked as a carpenter. Edward had two brothers Samuel and Nathan. The mother turned the boys over to the CAS while she was living with Mrs. Rachel Ackerman, Valhalla, N.Y. On March 13, 1914, he was placed in the home of Peter and Tillie Jorgeuson who resided two miles north and five miles east of Mitchell, S.D. at RFD #5. The Jorgeusons lived on a rented 160-acre farm one mile from the local school and attended the Lutheran church. On November 16, 1916, he then was placed in the home of Thomas Nerland, which was located three miles east of Parkston, S.D. Mr. Nerland owned a 160-acre farm. The Nerland's adopted him on December 29, 1916. In 1917 they moved to Rue Heights, S.D.

Spencer, Iowa
1914 Committee
Rev. Band, Methodist Episcopal
J.H. McCord, Banker
T.H. Johnson, Medical Doctor
H.L. Moulton, Merchant
Charles H.E. Leech, Hardware

Archibald Allen, case number 9531, was born in Benson Mines, N.Y. on April 1, 1912. His father worked as a laborer, his parents were Joseph T. and Maggie (Burnham) Allen. The CAS worker picked him up from the United Helpers Home and placed him with Oscar Johnson on December 10, 1914. Jr. Johnson lived five miles southwest of the depot in the town of Spencer, Iowa.

Anna Ericson, case number 9533, was born in N.Y.C. on May 21, 1908. Her mother was from Finland. Her father worked as a carpenter. They were Andrew and Emma Ericson. Anna was placed in the Five Points House of Industry. Emma lived at 109 St. Anns Avenue, N.Y.C. On November 24, 1914, Harlan James Buck took her in, residing at 347 West 4th Street, Spencer, Iowa.

Mr. Buck was an attorney and owned an eight-room farmhouse near the school.

Torvo Erkkanen, case number 9534, was born on December 15, 1908, in N.Y.C. to Gustave and Elizabeth (Autia) Erkkanen. Gustave had worked as a laborer and died. Elizabeth was living with Col. Robinson and turned Torvo over to the CAS workers on February 3, 1917. Elizabeth's address was 307 Prospect Avenue, Hackensack, N.J. Torvo was placed with August Grath who lived six miles southwest of Spencer, Iowa at RFD #1. Mr. Grath owned a 160-acre farm living in an eight-room house. They lived one and a half miles from the school and attended the Methodist Episcopal Church.

Gertrude Hulbert, case number 8889, was born to Clinton and Theresa Hulbert. Notes indicate that the parents abandoned her. There is no birthdate listed, she is attending the first grade in the spring of 1917. Gertrude was put in the care of Thomas Mathison living in Spencer, Iowa. Mr. Mathison owned 80-acres and worked farming. They lived in a six-room house one and a half mile from the school, were Lutheran's and had one boy.

Edna Kalnick, case number 8937, was born in N.Y. on October 3, 1912. Her father worked as a lumberman; he was Vasil Delso. Her mother was Mary Kalnick. Edna was city number A-6362, had disease of Eczema. A friend of the family was Mrs. Rader who lived at 719 East 3rd Street, N.Y.C. Edna was placed in the New York Nursery and Children's Hospital. On October 24, 1914, she was put in the care of Edward Benton Squire who lived on North Main Street, Spencer, Iowa. Mr. Squire worked as a clerk, owned a ten-room house eight-blocks from the school and attended the Methodist Episcopal church.

Laura May Long, case number 9538, was born in Geneva N.Y. on June 5, 1907. (Laura was baptized.)
Ruth Naomi Long, case number 9539, was born in Geneva, N.Y. on February 15, 1911.
Their parents were John H. and Helen (Curtain) Long. John occupation was a machinist. The parents last known to been living in Rochester, N.Y. and are intemperate. The girls were surrendered by S.P.C.C. and placed in the Ontario Orphan Asylum.

Laura was put in the care of Charles E. Leach, who lived five blocks from the depot at 243 West 5th Street, Spencer, Iowa. Mr. Leach worked as a merchant owning a twelve-room house two blocks from the school. He was of the Congregational faith.

Ruth, went to live with Willaim Castendych on October 24, 1917. The Castendych's owned an eight-room house at 426 West 5th Street, two blocks from the school and also attended the Congregational church.

Alfred Platt, case number 9540, was born in Pennsylvania on October 19, 1908. He was born to Alfred and Sarah (Robinson) Platt. Alfred (the father) deserted the family and Sarah then remarried. Alfred (the son) had been baptized. On November 25, 1914, he was placed in the home of Thomas P. Mathison seven miles southwest of Spencer, S.C. at RFD #2. Mr. Mathison worked as a farmer, owned 80-acres, and lived in a seven-room home. They resided one and a half miles from the school and are of the Lutheran faith.

Edward Strun, case number 9543, has no information regarding his age or parents. He is living with Mr. C.J. Griggs in Spencer, Iowa on May 5, 1917. Edward is working for Will Loucks under the direction of Mr. Griggs. Mr. Loucks lives three miles west and five miles north of Spencer. Iowa.

Bertha Horn Warren, case number 9608, was born in Baltimore on January 1, 1911. Her father was a sailor and is A.T. Horn. Her mother is Lillian Warren. Bertha's parents abandoned her, so she became a ward of the city, being placed in the New York Nursery and Children's Hospital. She was placed in the care of August W. Grath who lived 6-miles southwest of Spencer, Iowa at RFD #1. Mr. Grath worked farming, owned 160-acres and a seven-room home. The family was of the Methodist Episcopal faith and resided one and a half miles from the school.

Strawberry Point, Iowa
September 19, 1905
Walter Kingsland, case number 3654, was born in Brooklyn on August 31, 1901. His parents were of the Protestant faith living in Fireman, N.Y. they were Frank and Alice E. (Potter) Kingsland.

His mother was originally from Pennsylvania. Walter is city number 2584 and was placed at the Five Point House of Industry on May 19, 1905. On September 19, 1905, he was put in the care of Edward T. Partch. The Partch's lived two and a half miles southwest in Mederville, Iowa. Mr. Partch owned and farmed 70-acres a half mile from the local school. The family was of the Baptist faith and had two children. In July 1914, they moved into the town of Strawberry Point, Iowa eight and a half blocks east of the depot.

Sumner, Iowa
Nathan Smith, case number 9143, has no birthdate listed. (See brothers Edward Smith.) He was picked up from the mother in Valhalla, N.Y. and placed in the household of Frederick Bales of RFD Sumner, Iowa.

Charles Baldwin, case number 8426, was born on September 9, 1903, at Bellmore, Long Island. Both his parents were born in the United States. He was the son of David and Jennie (Burch) Baldwin. His father worked as a painter. The notes indicate that the father "disowns him." He was in the Home for Destitute Children. On November 13, 1912, went to live with Frank Paulson who lived five miles northeast of Clear Lake, Iowa at RFD #1 Mason city, Iowa. Mr. Paulson worked as a farmer; he owned 80-acres of land and rented an additional 80-acres. They live one and a half miles from the school. On June 20, 1913, he is then placed with J.F. Galford who resided at RFD in Thornton, Iowa. Mr. Galford rented 300-acres that he farmed. He lived one mile from the school and had three girls. The CAS went to make a visit on May 12, 1917, and listed him as a "Run Away".

Waterloo, Iowa
Francis Hedge, there is no information other than living with F.L. Benedict at 319 Highland Blvd. Waterloo, Iowa.

Hilding Anderson, case number 9498, was born in Sweden on January 26, 1901. His parents were Charles and Hilda Anderson. They lived at 111 East 128th Street, N.Y.C. and once Hilda died Hilding was sent to the Five Points House of Industry. In the Spring of 1916 Fred H. Kehr took Hilding in. The Kehr family lived six miles north at RFD #1, Waterville, Iowa. Mr. Kehr rented 120-acres, working as a farmer, they lived in a six-room house. The home is located a half mile from the school, they were of Lutheran faith and had a baby of their own.

Waukon, Iowa
Committee
I.E. Beeman, Mayor
E.B. Gibbs, Manager Electric Company
Dr. P.H. Letourneau, Physician
A.T. Nierling, Banker
Dr. A. T. Stillman, Dentist
C.H. Hale, Merchant

Erma Wilson, case number 10875, was born in Macedon, N.Y. on June 30, 1915. Her parents Archie and Hattie (Peeters) Wilson, are both from Fairport, N.Y. Mom "dropped dead" and Erma was put in charge of A. Steiger, Overseer of Poor in Macedon, N.Y. On May 11, 1919, she was taken in by John C. Rumph who lived eight miles southeast of Waukon, Iowa at RFD. The Rumph family consisted of a 12-year-old and lived three quarter miles from the school in a six-room house. Mr. Rumph worked as a farmer and owned 120-acres.

Oscar Benche, case number 8957, was born on March 7, 1907, in Denmark to Conrod and Maria (Naverro) Benche. His father died in Denmark and mother died in this country. Oscar's city number was A-708. Oscar was in the Home for Destitute Children and came to the CAS on October 14, 1913. His maternal grandfather, Raphael Navarro, lived in Montclair, N.J. On November 13, 1913, he was placed in the home of John C. Rumph. (See Erma Wilson's record.)

William Francis Burkhardt, case number 8428, was born in N.Y.C. on February 5, 1904. He was the son of William and Anna Burkhardt. Both parents were from N.Y.C. and his father was a Piano Worker. Notes indicate he had a brother George and was put in the Half Orphan Asylum on April 27, 1910. On November 13, 1912, he was taken in by Ray A. Tuthill. The home was at 726 South Madison, in Mason City, Iowa. Mr. Tuthill was a Brickmaker and rented a cottage near the local school. On December 27, 1913, William was then taken in by Ferdinand Burge residing 7-miles northwest of Luana, Iowa. The Burge house consisted of five-rooms, and they owned a 90-acre farm.

They lived a half mile from the school, attended the Presbyterian church and had a 1-year-old girl.

Gilbert Eadie, case number 8818, was born in N.Y.C. on November 11, 1902.

Walter Eadie, case number 8819, was born on December 8, 1904. Their parents were of Scottish heritage. Their father John was a stone cutter, and mom had died and there is no mention of her name. John was in the Tubercular Ward in Bellevue Hospital where he died. The boys were turned over to the CAS workers from Mrs. Jennings of 44 East 80th Street, N.Y.C. On January 24, 1914, both boys went to live with Dan Kelly who lived ten miles south and three miles east of Waukon, Iowa at RFD #1, Waterville, Iowa. The Kellys owned their farm and a ten-room house one and a half mile from the school and attended the Presbyterian Church.

Helen Kench, case number 8960, was born in Brooklyn on September 20, 1903. She was the daughter of Henry and Josephine (Sullivan) Kench. Her father died and she was put in the Sterling Place Home on October 14, 1913. She had an older sister, Mrs. Adams, whose address is unknown. On November 24, 1913, she was placed in the home of George Thompson residing nine miles southeast of Waukon, Iowa at RFD #3. Mr. Thompson worked farming, had 200-acres and a nine-room house. They lived one mile from the school and were of the Lutheran faith. Then Helen went to live with Mary A. Larson a half mile west of Lansing, Iowa at RFD #3. The Larsons farmed and owned 18-acres and a six-room home a half mile from the school. On February 20, 1918, Helen stayed with O.W. Johson in Lansing, Iowa before being placed in the home of John Turner on March 28, 1918. Mr. Turner resided in Chester, Iowa. Last she went back to live with George Thompson family in Waukonon June 18, 1918.

Hannah Miller, case number 8891, was born December 12, 1912, to Charles and Anna Miller. Mr. Miller worked as a driver. Hannah was placed in the Five Point House of Industry on June 3, 1913. She went to live with Jacob Schneider's family five miles north of Waterville, Iowa at RFD #2. The family farmed and owned a 160-acre and a five-room house. They lived a half mile from the school and were of the Lutheran faith.

Theodore Partington, case number 8824, was born in Peekskill, N.Y. on February 10, 1901. He was the son of James William and Ella (Smith) Partington of Marlborough, N.Y. James turned him over to the CAS after his mother died. On May 22, 1915, he was taken in by Otto A. Hanson who lived five miles north of Waterville, Iowa at RFD #2. The family consisted of a three-year-old boy and a one-year-old girl. They owned 163-acres farming a quarter mile from the school and attended the Lutheran church.

Francis Reihl, case number 8963, was born at Mt. Vernon on December 1, 1905. (Twin)
Helen Reihl, case number 8964, was also born at Mt. Vernon on December 1, 1905. (Twin)
Josephine Reihl, case number 8965, has no birth information available. (In 1917 she was in the sixth grade.) The children were born to Ferdinand and Mary (Younkers) Reihl. Mary is listed as immoral. They were taken to the CAS by Louis Clark, Commissioner of Charities.

Francis was placed in the home of Henry Sunderman who lives seven miles west of Waukon, Iowa at RFD #4. Mr. Sunderman worked farming and owned 200-acres and a nine-room house. They resided a quarter mile from the school and were of the Lutheran faith and the family had three girls.

Helen and Josehine were taken in on November 17, 1917, by John Buntrock. The Buntrock's lived in a nine-room house, owned 200-acres and were of the Methodist faith. They farmed, had three boys, and lived one and a half miles from the school.

Mildred Reynolds, case number 9043, was born in Massena, N.Y. on May 18, 1900. She was the daughter of Frank and Elizabeth (Kirby) Reynolds. Frank worked as a Paper Hanger and Decorator. Mildred was picked up by the CAS from the United Helpers Home in Ogdensburg, N.Y. She first went to live with Willington Lewis who resided three and a half miles east of Orchard, Iowa at RFD #3. Mr. Lewis farmed living in a ten-room house and owned 320-acres. The home was one mile from the school, and they attended the Methodist Episcopal church.

Henry Schaeffer, case number 8966, was born in Brooklyn on January 2, 1899, the son of Edward and Mary Schaeffer. He was institutionalized at the E.D.I.S. On November 21, 1913, he was placed in the care of John Arnold. Mr. Arnold worked as a Stock Man and lived in the town of Waukon, Iowa. He owned 200-acres near the school.

Anna Travers, case number 8968, was born in N.Y.C. on August 23, 1899, the daughter of Benjamin and Catherine Travers. Mr. Travers worked as a Steam Fitter. She was a ward of the city and in the Five Points House of Industry. On August 16, 1916, she was placed with Mrs. George Leppert who lived 10-miles north of Waukon at RFD #1 church, Iowa. The Leppert family owned 330-acres and a ten-room house. Mr. Leppert worked farming, and they lived a half mile from the school and attended the Methodist Episcopal church. They had four children in the family.

Anna Veritzan, case number 8800, was born on March 10, 1905, in Brooklyn. Her parents were Oscar and Annie (Smith) Veritzan. The father's whereabouts are unknown. The CAS picked her up from the Orphan Asylum Society. On April 8, 1915, she joined the Benjamin Peterson family ten miles east and a little south of Waukon, Iowa at RFD #3. Mr. Peterson works farming his 112-acre and lives in a seven-room home. They live three quarter miles from the school, of the Lutheran faith and have a 21-year-old child of their own.

West Branch, Iowa

Ernest Schmidt, case number 3517, was born in the United States on March 18, 1903, to German immigrants Godfry and Minnie E. (Dust) Schmidt. The family lived in Walton, N.Y. and Ernest had a brother and two sisters, Bertha, Carl, & Clara. Godfry worked as a laborer, while Minnie was in the Wayne County Alms House in Lyons, N.Y. She was in very poor health and suffered from an amental condition. On June 27, 1905, Ernest is placed with Mrs. Sarah F. Koch living in the town of Gallatin, Missouri. Mrs. Koch is a widow who owns her home and has one gown son. She lives near the local school. On October 24, 1907, Ernest is then in the home of J.B. Overfelt residing five miles north and two miles two west of Duncans Bridge, Missouri. The Overflet's live one and a half mile from the school and has two children. Then on December 11, 1908, J.P. Stotler takes Ernest in living eight miles northeast of West Branch, Iowa at RFD #3. The Stotler's own 400-acres and farms, living in a large house. They have two children and live one and a quarter mile from the school.

Carrie Volkert, case number 8435, was born on October 29, 1901, in Brooklyn. She was surrendered by her father who lived at 143 Cooper Street, Brooklyn, N.Y. after her mother died. The parents were William L. and Margaret (Geltner) Volkert. On October 28, 1916, she was placed in the care of Johnson Spear in the town of Tipton, Iowa. Mr. Spear is a retired farmer living in a nine-room house near the school and attends the Methodist Episcopal church. In July of 1917 she then goes to live with Mrs. L.H. Padellford, also living in Tipton, Iowa. Mr. Padellford is employed by the waterworks and lives in an eight-room house near the school. He also attends the Methodist Episcopal church and has a son aged twenty-eight.

Anna Kacin, case number 10472, was born November 19, 1906.
Joseph Kacin, case number 10473, was born September 30, 1905.
(See their sister Bertha and Louise Kacin.)
Anna was placed on January 29, 1917, in the care of J.J. Howard, two and a half miles from Zearing, Iowa.

Joseph was placed in the care of J.J. Howard who lived in a six-room house and rented 160-acres three and a half miles southwest of Zearing, Iowa.

Inas Eckerson, case number 10214, was born on September 8, 1902, in Schoharie, N.Y. to Charles and Mary (Manchester) Eckerson. Charles worked as a farm laborer and was killed by a bull. Mary is immoral. Clyde Proper, District Attorney of Schoharie County took custody of Inas. She was taken in by Henry Erickson who lived two and a half miles southeast of Zearing, Iowa. The family lived one and a quarter mile from the school. Mr. Erickson worked farming and rented 80-acres and lived in a six-room house.

Bryon Watson, case number 10515, was born in Russell, N.Y. on March 17, 1912. (See bother Evert) He also had a brother Glen. Bryon was first placed with Robert Louis Hertel on March 2, 1917. Mr. Hertel lived ten miles west and one and a half miles south of Rockland, Iowa. He is a Methodist Minister. On July 19, 1917, he was taken in by Ray E. Tight who lives two miles north and one and a half miles east of Yearling, Iowa, RFD. Mr. Tight farms 240-acres that he rents. The house consisted of nine-rooms, three quarter miles from the school and attend the Presbyterian church.

Bibliography

- Chalkboard Champions – Copyright © 2012 by Terry Lee Marzell, Chapter 6, Clara Comstock
- Natalle Cobb, Niece of Clara Comstock: Dunedin, Florida
- Crooked Lake Review, Spring 1999 "My Story" – Copyright © 1999 by Richard Call
- The Wichita Eagle (Wichita, Kansas) December 22, 1979. Copyright © 2022 by Newspaper.com
- Family of Elise May and Mary Elizabeth Turner: *Mary Burgh & Nancy Harding*
- Family of Samual Geleta: *Roseanne Testani Wall*
- The Goldfinch, Spring 2000, Vol. 21, No. 3, Iowa History for Young People
- Chicago Daily Times, 1939
- Missouri Valley Special Collection: Biography, Kansas City Library, Kansas City, kchistory.com
- http://dlib.nyu.edu/findingaids/html/nyhs/ms111_childrens_aid_society
- https://www.nyhistory.org/library
- Brace Memorial Farm School info@westchesterhistory.com
- https://fultonhistory.com
- https://ident.familysearch.org
- NYHS Reference reference@nyhistory.org
- www.orphantraindepot.com/ChildrensAidSociety History.html

Index

112

S Cotton History

Steve Cotton
Historian

Other books by this author.

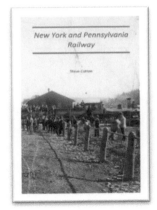

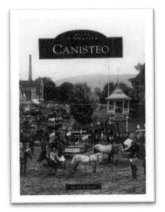

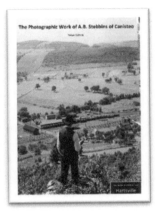

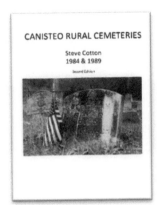

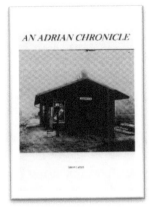

Back Cover:

The railroad tracks along the Canisteo River traveling through Steuben County, New York.